Journey to Joy

From Spiritual Rigidity to Freedom
A Spiritual Autobiography
2nd Edition

Ronald (Al) Rauckhorst
(With Contributions by Louise Rauckhorst)

Journey to Joy
Copyright 2024 by Ronald (Al) Rauckhorst

Inquiries and Book Orders should be addressed to:

Great Writers Media
Email: info@greatwritersmedia.com
Phone: 877-556-0487

ISBN: 979-8-89175-128-6 (sc)
ISBN: 979-8-89175-129-3 (ebk)

FIRST EDITION DEDICATION

To my wife, Louise
and to our daughters, Ann and Lisa,
who have been such great companions and
have shared so much of this *Journey to Joy*.

To all the wonderful people I have met and
walked with, some for just a short time
and others for significant and lasting
friendships, during my 89-year journey. The journey
road has been challenging, but never lonely.

SECOND EDITION DEDICATION

To the memory of
Ronald (Al) Rauckhorst,
a man of great faith
who learned well how to
"fall upward" on
his journey to joy.

ACKNOWLEDGMENTS

A HEARTFELT THANKS TO CAROL ZIMMERMAN, THE VON Raesfeld Agency, Henderson, NV for her immense help in making the 1st edition of this autobiographical work publishable.

To Louise Rauckhorst for her loving, generous support and editorial feedback throughout the 1st edition writing process.

To Sandy Martin for her editorial skills in preparation of both the 1st and 2nd editions.

To Marilyn McCartney, Kathy Futa, Barb Witt, Suzanne Corey, Rev. Linda Pilato and my fellow writers in the Anthem Authors Club for their encouragement, feedback and support.

To Janet Frischmon, Kathy Futa and Lyn Feliciano for their encouragement, feedback and support in preparation of the 2nd edition.

Louise and I owe each of them many, many thanks.

PREFACE to 2nd Edition

I BELIEVE THAT MY HUSBAND, RONALD (AL) RAUCKHORST, wrote the first edition of his book *Journey to Joy: From Spiritual Rigidity to Freedom* because, in sharing how his life experiences helped him to become a more open-minded, flexible, and loving person, he wanted to encourage readers of his book to become more open and loving in their relationships with other persons and with God. He wrote a very honest account of his amazing life and hoped that sharing it would encourage others on their life journeys.

I have felt impelled to publish this second edition of Al's book to tell, in Louise's Epilogue, how he spent his retirement years living out his personal creed (presented in Chapter Nine), and how he continued to transform the life challenges he faced during those years into opportunities to grow in love and grace.

The way Al lived his life showed that he kept learning to "fall upward", as described by Father Richard Rohr in his book *Falling Upward: A Spirituality for the Two Halves of Life* (Jossey Bass, 2011: San Francisco). The term "falling upward' refers to the universal pattern of loss and renewal in nature and literature—the supposed achievements of the first half of life (our survival dance) have to fall apart, be lost or we won't open up and move forward into our sacred dance in the second half of life.

The experiences of loss or falling Al lived through in his childhood, his Maryknoll years, his years as a husband and father, and his years trying with limited success to establish a successful career path after he left the active priesthood—as well as the declines he faced in old age—all became for Al ways to "fall upward", to grow spiritually through imperfection, through cycles of loss and renewal in his life circumstances.

St. Paul expressed his "falling upward" this way: ". . . but he [the Lord] said to me. "My grace is sufficient for you, for power is made perfect in weakness." I will rather boast most gladly of my weaknesses, in order that the power of Christ may dwell in me. Therefore, I am content with weaknesses, insults, hardships, persecutions, and constraints, for the sake of Christ, for when I am weak, then I am strong." (2 Corinthians 12: 9-10)

I have also added a few stories and some of my own perspectives in the Chapters that describe the parts of Al's life journey that I had the good fortune to share. I hope they will help to further illuminate the life journey of a wonderful human being.

Louise Rauckhorst

Note: Al's family always called him by his first name, Ronald, but he preferred that his friends called him "Al" , a shortening of his middle name, Albert. This is why I refer to him as Al throughout my additions to this second edition of his book.

Contents

CHAPTER 1

Getting to Know Me

I WAS AN AVERAGE GUY WHO BELIEVED HE lived an extraordinary life. I came to earth with a purpose and believed I lived so as to attain it. It has been a truly amazing journey! I believed that, as spiritual beings who temporarily live in a human body, we have made a sacred contract with God to be born. This is a belief that thousands share and perhaps millions do not.

We learn through the human experience of each successive life what our soul needs to grow in love. Although most of us are ordinary and don't have the potential to be a Mozart or an Einstein, we all have the potential to live extraordinary lives of love. Understanding that gives meaning to our lives.

I knew that attaining a greater knowledge of God enabled me to grow in the love of God and my neighbor. That doesn't necessarily mean that I reached any great level of love, only that I learned to love more than I did before I was born into this life.

I started out this life as a very narrow-minded, rigid thinker, fitting everything neatly into concrete, black and white categories. I was born the fourth of five children. My parents were very religious Roman Catholics. As a young child I learned that the Church and my parents were to be obeyed. If I didn't obey my parents, disapproval and punishment would be incurred and disobeying the Church would incur eternal damnation.

On the other hand, by obeying I would become a good person, especially pleasing to my parents and to God. I didn't learn to distinguish between light, serious, and very serious commands or between just and unjust ones. I simply bought the whole package. Obeying them all was my way to be safe. It would enable me to become a good person headed for heaven.

A deep fear of not doing so and ending up in hell for eternity was a strong motivating factor throughout my first thirty-five years. My parents, the Church and I, myself, used fear and guilt as motivating factors automatically. It wasn't a conscious decision. It was just the way it was.

I'm not complaining. My parents and family were very good for me. I guess that's why I chose them as part of my sacred contract. My childhood was good, not perfect. I inherited a strong case of introversion from my mother which put us on the same wavelength. My father was an extrovert, which left me feeling that he didn't understand me. Isn't that a common kid's complaint about a parent, or even a spouse about a spouse?

I identified with my mother, a quiet woman who seldom verbalized her beliefs, religious or otherwise, but surely lived them. If she did verbalize a belief, it meant that it was an especially strong one. One belief that meant a lot to me was my mother saying that we were to decide our own future, to become what we wanted to be. When I was ordained a priest, she supported me completely (as did my father).

Ten years later she accepted my decision to leave the active priesthood without judging me. It hurt her, I'm sure. She said she just couldn't understand how I went from being a very happy, committed priest to becoming a very angry, former priest. At the time, I couldn't explain it either. Because I had grown a beard, my mother thought I was trying to be a "beatnik". At the time, I didn't even know what being a "beatnik" meant. I was just enjoying my freedom to be me.

My father never showed me his disappointment when I left the priesthood. His only comment was that he hoped I would be able to settle down. It was only many years after he died that my brother told me he had cried.

I met many women after I left the priesthood, but none of the relationships really clicked . . . then I met Louise. I was in awe. It felt so extraordinarily exciting to be in her company or to walk down the street with her. I was always at ease when I was with her. I understood her caution about entering into an intimate relationship so soon after leaving religious life, and when I didn't "get it" she would tell me. Thank God I listened!

Throughout fifty years of marriage we have had some serious disagreements, but nothing we haven't been able to work out. Our political, religious, parental, and psychological beliefs complemented each other and helped us to grow together.

One of our few areas of disagreement has been financial. Louise is a careful, savvy buyer. She checks the sales and clips coupons. She will make the extra effort and go out of her way to purchase an item a little cheaper. She feels foolish paying more for an article than is absolutely necessary. I, on the other hand, could have cared less about shopping around for the best bargains.

The amazing thing was that, when the occasion arose, Louise didn't shrink away from very expensive purchases, like buying a house, a car, or furniture. She enjoyed it. It was like an adventure and she'd be off in pursuit. She compares and looks at everything available to make sure she's getting a good buy and then she signs on the dotted line.

If there's an obstacle, Louise doesn't get angry. She just backs up, considers the whole situation, and works out a solution. Finally, she works hard to back up her commitment. A Vedic astrologer once told her that she would never have a problem earning money. In her high school yearbook Louise was noted as "most sophisticated." She is, but it's so natural. She doesn't act it. She's not aware of it. She's just herself.

I had a habit of teasing Louise but sounding very serious. Fortunately for me, Louise never took me seriously and simply laughed or ignored me. It's one of her wonderful traits that I loved and appreciated. It's also an example of how we always seemed to understand each other.

When I would say something outrageous to Louise in my mother's presence she never commented or intervened, but she would give me a look that said it all: How can you say such a terrible thing to such a kind and beautiful woman like Louise? Do you know what you are doing?

My father died shortly after I met Louise. He never met her, but I am sure that he would have loved her—he was a sucker for a pretty face! My mother lived ten years longer. We stayed with her whenever we visited family in Akron, Ohio.

I was a rather colossal failure as an income earner. I was never able to match my education and talent to earning income. After leaving the priesthood, I wasn't able to function at the work for which I was trained; nor could I ever get too excited about earning more money. I was too introverted and was never able to acquire the skills needed in a business environment.

However, I worked hard and did some good work. The Vedic astrologer, mentioned in relation to Louise's good fortune with earning money, informed me that the position of the planet Saturn in my astrological chart indicated that I would always face obstacles regarding career and income.

After leaving the priesthood I worked as: a psychology intern at a children's psychiatric hospital; a youth and family counselor; a sales rep (though I never sold anything); an advisor for college minority students (a great job); a tutor for elementary and high school kids; plus doing some less-demanding jobs as well.

Louise taught nursing students in various universities. When we got married she moved from the Boston area to New York City where I was working and taught at the Beth Israel School of Nursing and at Lehman College. Six years later I followed her back to Boston, and then to Baltimore, Boston again, Oshkosh, and San Diego. I needed to find work in each location before we retired to the Las Vegas area.

Finding work was always stressful for me. For Louise, finding jobs was not difficult but the work itself could be very stressful. As the primary bread-winner, she felt obligated to stay in certain positions where she was overworked and under-appreciated.

REAL LIFE ETHICAL DILEMMAS

We married in July 1971, when I was thirty-eight and Louise was thirty-six—shortly before our next birthdays. We wanted children, but it took over four years before Louise became pregnant. Being a nurse, she was well aware of the dangers of pregnancy for older women.

In our case, this became a reality. An ultrasound analysis showed that our baby had Cat-Eye Syndrome (also known as Schmid-Fraccaro syndrome). Cat-Eye syndrome is a very rare genetic disorder that occurs sporadically in people with no family history of the condition. It gets its name from the distinctive eye pattern (which resembles a cat's eye) present in many affected individuals. And it is characterized by abnormal development of the eyes, ears, mouth, anal region, heart and/or kidney of the affected fetus. The prognosis was that our baby would be mentally retarded, require multiple infant surgeries for heart and genital malformations, and have a short lifespan.

Louise and I cried. We agonized. We were broken-hearted. We wanted this baby very much. We researched medical and ethical sources, including moral theologians, and consulted people we trusted. Believing in the Church's teaching on the primacy of the individual conscience, we finally decided that Louise would have an abortion.

Having worked in a children's psychiatric hospital, I had seen too many small children basically beyond any help, who spent their entire day crying and literally banging their heads against the wall. Besides the fact that our baby would probably be too much for us to care for psychologically, emotionally, as well as financially, we came to believe it wasn't right to birth such an infant to a short life of surgery and suffering.

As devout Catholics, this decision flew in the face of all we had been taught. In Roman Catholic doctrine, it was God's will that we have the baby. An abortion was opposing God's will and committing murder. But we also believed that God gave us intelligence and expected us to use it. God left the decision to us. What was the best decision in this case?

There is no certainty that we decided "correctly" or in accordance with God's will, just the certainty that it was our decision to make according to our own consciences. We have lived with this uncertainty without regret, believing in the Church's doctrine of the primacy of individual conscience, and trusting in God who trusted us in giving us free will. It also brought it home to us that doctrine in the abstract is quite different than actually living in a difficult situation and having to make a no-win decision.

There are so many areas of life like this that are not black or white, but ambiguous shades of grey. They are the situations where you feel there is no winning solution. Whichever way you decide involves hurt and loss. You can only accept the uncertainty and make the best decision you can, trusting that our merciful God will respect our conscience, our intentions, and the intelligence He/She gave us.

So, it was with our baby. Though undesirable in itself, we believed that abortion was best for the baby, for us, and for society. At the same time, it was a terrible loss. For two or more years, Louise avoided looking at mothers with infants and small children. It hurt too much. We never really stopped grieving and would choke up when talking about the baby we lost. But we also looked forward to meeting our baby in the next life. We believed that she attained her purpose in agreeing to become a deformed fetus that would be aborted. We believed that this was a courageous act on her part and that she did it with love. We hoped we acted with love as well.

Note that it is easy to accept Church doctrine in the abstract. Accepting it in the "concrete" of actual personal experience, however, is something else. Yet ethical dilemmas can be blessings in disguise. They force us to be open to change. For Louise and I, the abortion decision was an example of this. It forced us to follow our conscience and decide for ourselves, even in opposition to Church doctrine.

It was helpful to know that even a great theologian like St. Thomas Aquinas taught that one may not act against one's conscience in order to follow a Church teaching. This doesn't mean that we recommend abortion. We definitely believe that all life is sacred. In many cases, but not all, we have still opposed abortion; yet, we have respected the woman's right to decide. Ultimately, she has to make the decision and take responsibility for it.

We knew that there were many Catholics and Church hierarchs who would condemn our actions. We respected objections from those who have experienced similar ethical situations and decided differently. We also knew that there are many Catholics today who have experienced the same kind of dilemma and arrived at the same conclusion; but in today's atmosphere, no one feels it is safe to talk about it.

Another example of an ethical dilemma that forces decisions and can change people's beliefs is the controversy over homosexuality. It can be easy for some people and church authorities to call homosexual activity an "inherent evil" — that is, until people discover that their own son or daughter, or another loved one, is homosexual. They know in their gut that their son or daughter or other loved one is not inherently evil or disordered.

This created an ethical dilemma for some parents I knew who discovered their child was gay. One couple recognized that their son was not inherently evil or disordered. They accepted their child as he was and questioned the Church's teaching. They could not condemn the child they loved or force him to change.

Another couple set out to change their child. They sent him to aversion therapy. For a short period after the therapy, he tried to live as his parents wanted. But within a few weeks he was back living with his male friends. His parents were not able to question their church's teaching and could not accept their son's behavior. This left them feeling helpless and unhappy with their son. They felt compelled to find a way to "save" their son.

A greater dilemma: What if you are homosexual? You didn't choose to be such, no more than heterosexuals choose their sexual orientation. You were born that way. One gay priest friend in San Diego told me that people will sometimes ask him, "When did you decide to become a homosexual?" His reply was always the same: "When did you decide to become a heterosexual?" In fact, science has discovered that there is a biological basis for homosexuality.

Fearing rejection by family, peers, and society, some gays/lesbians try to hide the fact or even deny it to themselves. They live with the fear that they will be found out. Some marry a heterosexual person to prove to themselves and others that they are not homosexual. Their life is a lie, an ethical dilemma.

They simply want to be themselves like everyone else and to share in loving relationships.

I believed that there were several in my rather large extended family back in Ohio who were gay and lesbian. They were afraid to say so and risk the family's disapproval, because most of my family members are very conservative in regard to both their religion and their politics.

Individuals who do "come out" frequently find that, in accepting themselves as they are, they are stronger and more at peace with themselves. In resolving the dilemma, they have matured, and believe it or not, they have grown spiritually. Now the dilemma is passed on to those around them and they, in turn, must resolve it. Unfortunately, some Catholics are not able to question their blind obedience to the Church and choose to condemn and reject their child or loved one.

I have a priest classmate who was not able to announce publicly that he was gay until our 50th class reunion. By then he was in his seventies. He was a very good priest and remained celibate all his life.

Today transgender identity issues are at the forefront of the public debate in the United States and present serious challenges regarding how the Church will respond. Hopefully the Church will consider, not only relevant moral aspects and current scientific knowledge concerning gender, but also the pastoral approaches of compassion and mercy needed by those who are not comfortable with the gender assigned at their birth.

An ethical dilemma can be a great force for change and spiritual growth, but one must be open to change and have the ability to question one's own core beliefs. It is scary and far from easy. If you can't do it now, look out. As in the movie *Ground Hog Day*, you will have to keep coming back until you get it right.

I believed that most people act with good will and are trying to grow spiritually. In my case, this was why I entered the seminary, studied for nine years, was ordained and worked as a missionary priest in South Korea for almost ten years. . . and it is basically why I left Maryknoll and the active priesthood. I experienced the Roman Catholic Church as an institution more concerned with earthly goals and concerns than spiritual growth.

Because I was naïve, this surprised me. The Catholic hierarchy, as well as many priests, religious and lay persons would disagree with me. But so many of the Church's decisions have been based on what was good for the institution, to protect its reputation and its doctrine and dogmas. The child sex abuse scandal is one such example. Decisions were made to protect the reputation of the Church and its priests rather than the innocent victims of the abuse. The hierarchy consulted lawyers, not spiritual directors, in making decisions about how to respond to the crisis.

The hierarchy also continues to refuse to consider optional celibacy and the ordination of women to the diaconate and the priesthood. These are two more examples of the fact that the hierarchy also faces ethical dilemmas and, up to now, has been unable to change.

I have been asked if I would ever have returned to the active priesthood. I could not under the hier-archical clerical structure in today's Roman Catholic Church. I presided at some private Eucharistic cel-ebrations, having been asked to do so by other Catholics. This small Catholic community eventually came to realize, based on the teachings of sacra-mental theologians, that they could preside at the Eucharist themselves without an ordained priest. They came to realize that it is the Holy Spirit who causes Christ to be truly present in the Eucharist and in the community. The ordained priest may preside, but he doesn't perform any miracles.

There are, in fact, many such private Eucharistic celebrations quietly being performed without an ordained priest present. As one nun told me, "Let's gather and share bread and wine, and, who knows, maybe Jesus will join us."

DECIDING TO LEAVE THE PRIESTHOOD

Leaving the active priesthood was not easy. It took me two to three years to agonize my way through to the decision. In some ways, I compared it to marriage and divorce. I had committed myself for life to a celibate priesthood with a promise to obey my superiors. Initially, there was no problem. I was busy in South Korea and enjoyed the missionary life immensely. I felt I was doing what God wanted me to do.

Then the Second Vatican Council changed everything. The reforms it sought to bring about seemed to me to be so honest, so right on target to promote God's love and truth in the modern world. The teachings of Vatican II caused me to reflect on and seriously question my beliefs.

Implementing the reforms this Council envisioned involved changing age-old rules and behavior and beliefs. Too many in Church leadership didn't agree with the reforms. They must have felt as though they were losing "their" Church. So, I was forced to see beyond my naïveté and realize the hypocrisy and resistance to change within the Church.

Many in Church leadership didn't see the Vatican II reforms as contributing to the spiritual growth of the people, but rather saw them as a weakening of "their" Church. So "their" focus was on protecting the Church and (consciously or unconsciously) their own power and vested interests. I thought that they didn't distinguish between the Church as an institution and the Church as the People of God (as taught by the Council). The result has been a polarized Church and the blocking of implementation of the reforms envisioned by the Council fathers.

I was changing and many in Church leadership were not. What to do? My Maryknoll priest colleagues became divided, with some wanting change and others opposing change. Some of those wanting change decided there was no sense in waiting for change that wasn't about to happen, so they left the priesthood.

Others decided to stay and work for change within the Church. Many of these men also eventually left the priesthood, realizing that the Vatican hierarchy was just too opposed to change. But others remained and still supported the reforms of the Second Vatican Council as much as they could. They have been doing so in a Church environment that, at least up until the election of Pope Francis, increasingly seemed to be trying to dismantle those reforms.

Today Pope Francis is trying to get the Church to focus more on the travails of the poor and marginalized, with an emphasis on mercy versus adherence to strict doctrine. For example, he has stated that the Church should be viewed as a field hospital for the physically, mentally, emotionally and/or spiritually wounded in our midst. Pope Francis is aiming to create a more synodal Church wherein all the People of God, including the laity (and women), have a voice in decision-making. Unfortunately, he continues to experience a lot of resistance from certain cardinals, bishops, and other Catholic conservatives.

Mandatory celibacy for priests is one of the contentious issues in the Church, but I didn't think it was the main issue. For me, the main issue was the question of positive and long overdue change versus blind obedience to rules and regulations.

My dilemma was being caught between commitment to my priestly vows and my deep anger at a Church that often prioritizes its rules and regulations over the spiritual good of its people. I couldn't help equating the attachment of members of the hierarchy to their positions, their rules, doctrines, and pronouncements—their authority—to biblical Pharisaism. There are many selfless, dedicated priests and members of religious orders who are serving God and their fellow men in wonderful ministries. I admired them immensely, as well as the lay persons working alongside them.

I eventually came to the conclusion that I had two choices. If I stayed in the priesthood, I would be able to pat myself on the back when I died and tell God I had kept my priestly vows. Or I could leave and risk God's condemnation, trusting in His/Her compassion and mercy, and hope I was following the inspiration of the Holy Spirit. After I decided to leave the active priesthood, it took a couple of years to get a dispensation from the Vatican, at which time I was "reduced" to the status of a lay person. For me, it was a blessing in disguise. I was proud to be a lay person.

In the seminary, we were taught that ordination to the priesthood changed us ontologically. Our souls were indelibly marked and we were then essentially different from lay persons, different from the rest of mankind. This teaching came into being around the 12th century and was used to support the validity of the rule of mandatory celibacy. I didn't know of any clear evidence to support the claim that ordination changes a person essentially.

Unfortunately, this belief helped to produce the clerical caste, a system that puts priests on a pedestal and leads to them being treated differently from other people. Abuse of the clerical status and a devaluing of lay people has been a natural result.

The Church hierarchy generally treats laicized priests as second-class citizens and tries to treat them as if they don't exist. For example, they are not allowed to serve in any ministries in Catholic parishes. The negative treatment given to CORPUS (a national organization that advocates for a priesthood open to all whom God calls, regardless of gender, marital status or sexual orientation) and other international groups of formerly active priests is also a prime example of how those who have left the active priesthood are treated.

However, the priests I knew, and Maryknoll itself, treated me with respect and openness after I left the active priesthood. For example, I have been welcomed back to Maryknoll to celebrate ordination anniversaries. I have priest friends, but the Church hierarchy ignores laicized priests as a group.

I was very angry when I left Maryknoll and the active priesthood. Because of the depth of my anger, Maryknoll supported my decision to consult a psychiatrist of my choosing for a year after I left. When the year was up, I continued therapy for another two years on my own.

Dr. Edward Whitmont, a psychiatrist and Jungian analyst who I believed was Jewish, put me in touch with my shadow side, all the feelings I had rejected and repressed for most of my life. I really wasn't aware of my feelings.

During one group session, for example, I had a disturbing interaction with one of the women in the group. I left the session that afternoon feeling bothered, but not quite knowing why. That evening, while lying in bed just before falling asleep, it hit me. I was angry with that woman. She had rejected me. I couldn't believe it. The anger changed to joy as I finally understood what had been bothering me.

When I told Dr. Whitmont that it had taken me hours to realize I was angry, he replied that I was lucky because so many people go through life and never know that they're angry. I realized then that I had been repressing anger my whole life—since I was a child who was not allowed to be angry.

I had been taught by word and example that being angry was not being nice. Dr. Whitmont taught me that anger can be good when it arouses the energy to do something positive about whatever has been causing it. It was good for me to acknowledge my anger and use the energy it aroused to resolve the situation in a constructive way.

Another important insight was gained during a different group session when Dr. Whitmont commented that I was very judgmental. I thought he was way off the mark on that one, and was about to vociferously defend myself, when I noticed everyone in the group was nodding in agreement. That stopped me. I was forced to consider the possibility that I really was judgmental and my denial was a self-deceiving defense.

Working through the decision to leave the priesthood, together with my sessions with Dr. Whitmont, left me feeling like I was going through puberty again in my late thirties. I was finally growing up and would continue to be growing up for the rest of my life. But all of this trying to understand myself was hard work. Who wants to face up to all the flaws in one's personality? It was also an exciting and joyous adventure. Growing into maturity was what was necessary for me to grow spiritually in the knowledge and love of God.

Another of Dr. Whitmont's challenges that helped me immensely happened the day he asked me what I believed. I started telling him and he stopped me.

"No," he said. "That is what you were taught. I am asking what you believe."

This forced me to question everything, a scary task indeed. Suddenly I was naked—psychologically, emotionally, and spiritually. I could only answer that I believed in God. I couldn't say more. I knew God. Everything else about my faith had been taught to me. I was stripped of the foundation on which I had built my life.

I had not previously asked myself Dr. Whitmont's question, "What do I believe?" But I had asked it of one of my theology professors a year or so before meeting Dr. Whitmont. I was still in the process of leaving and had sought out my seminary dogma professor. I asked him about some of the questions I had about theology and then asked him what he believed. He gave me the basic "book" answers. I said that I was asking what he believed, not "book" answers, but he merely repeated his "book" answers.

I was disappointed. I knew the "book" answers. He never even said that he believed what the book said. That was all he would say. He never betrayed what he actually believed. My guess was that, in his position, he didn't want to be accused of teaching any heresy. He was expressing only blind, unquestioning acceptance of the standard teaching. In effect, he was saying, "Don't question, just believe."

But I was questioning and needed an honest, personal response from him. He couldn't give it. I have often wondered if he really was questioning but wasn't quite sure what he, himself, believed.

I think that dogma can be a great stumbling block. We get all absorbed in studying dogmas about God and ignore what the Christian mystics (like St. Francis, St. Teresa of Avila, St. John of the Cross and Meister Eckhart) teach us: that God is this awesome Being, this Spiritual Force of Light and Love, this Divine Presence who always with us.

I was left with a deep sense of joy and gratitude. I kept wanting to join all the saints, living and dead, and all the angels as they dance and sing their joyous hymns of praise and thanksgiving. As the Preface of the Mass says, "It is right to give Him thanks and praise."

Some people would surely question my faith stance. It must seem egotistical and heretical to those who are not able to question their own faith. I still considered myself a "faith-full" Catholic, although I disagreed with some of the "official" teachings of the Roman Catholic Church. I also knew that there were Catholic theologians, and even some bishops, who disagreed as well, but are reluctant to say so publicly.

I may sound like I was a "cafeteria Catholic," simply choosing to believe what I wanted to believe and ignoring the rest. Perhaps I have been misguided, but I experienced joy in my faith, my knowledge of God, and the freedom that flows from God's love. Giving up on the idea of making myself holy, accepting myself as I am, and trusting in God's love was enough.

If someone had wished to call me a heretic, so be it. If some Church leader wanted to ex-communicate me, I would have regretted it, but it wouldn't have changed my relationship with God.

St. Paul said it best: "For I am convinced that neither death, nor life, nor angels, nor principalities, nor present things, nor future things, nor powers, nor height, nor depth, nor any other creature will be able to separate us from the love of God in Christ Jesus our Lord" (Romans 8: 38-39).

St. Paul doesn't stop with the Pope—an office that didn't exist in his day anyway—he includes the angels and the entire spirit world, as well as all earthly creatures, as being unable to separate me from God.

CHAPTER 2

Growing Up

WHY HAVE I WRITTEN ABOUT MY PAST, unless to help explain the person I became? There have been so many factors and so many people who influenced me throughout my life. I felt sad that I often didn't remember them, their names, or what they specifically did that affected me in some special way.

My being born into a German Catholic family in Akron, Ohio explained a lot. My family was very religious and adherence to the Roman Catholic religion was strengthened by the traditional German trait of stubbornness and my parents' expectations of unquestioning obedience and discipline.

I was comfortable in this family environment. It made me aware of God's presence in my life. It made me feel special. I was always aware that, as Catholics, we were different from our neighbors. We were held to a higher standard. For example, we had to go to church every Sunday under pain of mortal sin. In some ways I envied Billy next door who didn't have to go to church.

Mom (Rose Bechter) and Dad's (Albert Rauckhorst) 1921 wedding portrait with flower girl. Aunt Josie & Uncle Clarence standing.

Growing up I always felt different and excluded from the experiences of the non-Catholics. Thus, I felt uncomfortable being among some non-Catholics and usually sought to avoid them. They wouldn't understand why I didn't feel free to do the things that they might do. Although this family and religious discipline was meant to protect me from experiencing evil behavior and worldly temptation, it also gave me a feeling of moral superiority and a fearful suspicion of whatever I might find in the secular world.

Me, in elementary school

This fear caused me to see evil out there in totally innocent behavior and situations. I later realized how irrational such fear can be because it is based on ignorance: that is, on evil imagined in my own mind and not based on reality. The fear of difference allows one to dismiss or exclude another without any actual evidence or experience of evil. It caused me to discriminate unfairly against innocent and truly wonderful people.

For example, I remember as a teenager reading about Reverend Martin Luther King, Jr. How stupid I was! I thought that anyone named after Martin Luther couldn't be all that good. To my way of thinking, Martin Luther was a heretic and against God, so Martin Luther King, Jr. must really be a heretic as well.

My childhood years were not unusual. I had two brothers and two sisters. My oldest sibling, Regina, was eight years older than me. Paul was six years older, Roseanna was four years older, and Bernard was two years younger than me.

Because of the age differences, Regina and Paul seemed like adults to me. They lived in another world. They were in high school and then Regina was off to work as a secretary at Firestone and Paul was drafted into the Army. He was on a World War II troop ship on his way to the Orient when Japan surrendered.

My other sister, Roseanna, did some nice things for Bernard and me, like organizing playtime. She also liked to boss Bernard and me around, especially to get the dishes and household chores done. Then she entered the convent in her freshman year of high school and she was gone.

Bernard and I were then the only children left at home, and we were close enough in age that we did almost everything together. When I finished high school and left for the seminary, I thought I would miss my parents the most. To my surprise, it was Bernard I missed the most. I enjoyed vacation times at home as long as he was around; otherwise, I was always ready to return to the seminary.

My parents certainly exerted a great influence on me. They were not highly educated, but they were quite intelligent. My mother completed 6th grade and then had to work. My father made it to the 9th grade.

My mother created a religious atmosphere in our home with holy pictures, statues, and prayer plaques. We were expected to be good and obey. Backtalk was never tolerated. I can't remember her ever striking me physically, although she did threaten to do so on occasion.

My dad was religious as well, but not quite as pious as my mother. Once in a while he would swear and was quickly reprimanded by my mother, who demanded that there be "none of that pit talk in our home." The pit she referred to was the Goodrich factory pit where tires were manufactured and where dad worked for most of his life. It was physically demanding and very dirty work. My father rarely talked about it, and he didn't complain.

Having barely survived the Depression in the 1930s, dad appreciated having a steady job. One of his frequent observations about me was that I didn't appreciate the value of a dollar. His assessment of me was correct at that time.

My father tried to watch his language in deference to my mother. One of his favorite sayings, especially aimed at other drivers, was "That horse's neck!" He's the only person I ever heard use that expression. This was an accommodation for my mother's sake, but it took years before I realized that the word "neck" was a substitute. As our canon law professor used to say, "There are more horses asses in the world than there are horses."

You can imagine my father's joy at hearing my mother tell the awning company, after repeated delivery delays, that they could "take that awning and stuff it." An hour later they arrived and put up the awning on the sunroom just in time for my mother's afternoon card club meeting. Dad just laughed and laughed, and then asked us, "Did she really say that?" It was probably the closest to swearing that mom ever got.

You can imagine the shock we all felt when Bernard came home from John Carroll University and reported that the Jesuit priest teaching religion told them it was okay to say "god damn." I had never heard that phrase uttered in our house. We were taught that this was a major misuse of God's name, a really offensive sacrilege God would take personally.

As my parents and I stood there with our mouths open, Bernard added ". . . provided you use a small letter 'g'." I wondered how you could know what size letter a person was using when he spoke. Some 50 years later, I was still uncomfortable with voicing that swear expression, although I had often thought it (with a small "g") whenever I was especially frustrated.

During my high school years dad kept Bernard and me busy helping him with home repairs and car maintenance chores, even with building a new house for our family. We also had to help with feeding the chickens. I drew the line at chopping their heads off when that time came.

The biggest trauma of my growing up years was being sexually molested by an older neighborhood boy. At 12 years of age, I was prepubescent. The molesta-

RONALD (AL) RAUCKHORST

tion happened over the course of one summer. This fellow inappropriately touched most of the boys in our immediate neighborhood. To our astonishment, he would often masturbate in front of us, touch our privates, and urge us to touch his. He talked constantly about sex. I learned a lot about sex that summer.

This behavior came to a screeching halt on the day this fellow touched a little two-year-old. The toddler's mother realized what had happened, confronted the boy's mother, and it all stopped. This boy was later drafted into the military, served during the Korean War, and never came home. He was listed as "missing in action." He might have been caught in the onslaught that occurred when the Chinese joined in that war.

At this point, my mother learned what had been going on. She was not good at handling sexual issues, but asked why I let him bother me. When I explained how he would hold me, she declared that this was a sin. That was the only time my mother ever talked about sex with me.

The only sex education I received from my father took place a couple of years later. Bernard and I slept in the same room. My dad came in and showed us a book with some terrible pictures of people with all sorts of ugly, sexually-transmitted diseases. He told us that this is what happens when you "fool around." And that was it.

Of course, being a very introverted teenager, I was embarrassed. Partly because of my past experiences and partly because my parents were uncomfortable talking about sex, I was happy that they never felt the need to go beyond those talks. I was

28

content with what I learned from my own reading and from my classmates and other kids. I looked all over the house for that book with the ugly disease pictures in it, but never found it.

I felt terribly ashamed about the molestation events. I had sinned. What could I do to repair my relationship with God? On the positive side, even at twelve years of age I was very certain that sex had to be a good thing. Wasn't this how babies got made and why people got married? Yet I felt that any participation on my part during the molestations was somehow wrong. It might be okay in marriage, but it certainly was not okay for us kids. It was only later, after I became pubescent, that I experienced the drive for sex and what a wonder sex could really be.

When talking about religious vocations, the nuns at school declared that the greatest aspiration a boy could have would be to become a priest. But they always added the qualification that you had to have a "calling." By that they meant God chose you to be a priest. You didn't choose this vocation for yourself.

Because I wanted to be as great a person as I could be, the idea of becoming a priest really attracted me and made me feel that I did have "the calling." I believed that this would also fulfill my need to repair my relationship with God. I would become a priest. I would answer the call.

I knew this would involve celibacy and decided that the best way to make up for my sin was to give up good sex, even though I really didn't know what that meant at that prepubescent age. I just knew there had to be such a thing as good sex free of sin.

So, I made a private vow to become a priest, having been taught in Catholic school that private vows to God were a serious matter. If you broke such a vow, you could expect to go to hell.

Not long ago, my brother Bernard, insisted that what had attracted me to becoming a priest was my desire for adventure. Reading books on adventure played a big part in my intellectual nourishment growing up. Bernard was right! I wanted to be part of a great adventure. I didn't think that becoming a priest was an adventure in itself, so I focused on becoming a Maryknoll priest who would strive to do God's good work in foreign lands. The prospect of going to some exotic foreign country made all the difference.

HIGH SCHOOL DAYS

I attended St. Mary's High School, as my older brother and sisters had done. Getting there usually required a mile walk and a 30-minute streetcar ride. There were times when I walked and times when a friend's father drove us to the streetcar stop. Later, another friend's father drove several of us all the way to school on his way to work at IBM.

Coming home, the mile walk was all uphill. We didn't give it much thought because we always had each other for company. I liked going to St. Mary's. I felt lucky to have avoided the non-religious public high school in Kenmore where we lived, which most of my grammar school classmates attended.

I enjoyed having interactions in high school with a larger number of classmates with different personalities, life experience, and world views. All the classes were taught by Dominican sisters from Monroe, Michigan. Sister Dominica, my aunt and my father's sister, was a member of that community. Fifteen or twenty years later, she taught at St. Mary's.

The sisters (or nuns) were good women. Some were exceptional teachers, but some were less adept in their teaching skills. The classes and all the social interactions were great learning experiences. But I had made my vow to become a priest and I was mostly interested in finishing high school and moving on to the seminary.

During Christmas vacation in my junior year, I remember considering suicide. The Christmas holidays were past and our vacation was nearly over. In my mind, all I could look forward to was a cold January and more school drudgery. I was also feeling overwhelmed with the demands of school and life in general.

I remember seriously considering suicide because it seemed like the quickest and easiest way to escape my current situation. But I also believed that, if I committed suicide, I would be spending an eternity in hell. So, suicide just would not work. From that day on, suicide was no longer an option for me.

I only thought about suicide just that one day. I must have been depressed, but I didn't realize this until years later. I remember riding the streetcar on the way to school later in January, telling my friends how I hated school but couldn't quit. I knew I had to get through high school before I could get on with my life.

It's interesting that I later came to no longer believe in hell and resented the Catholic Church having used fear of hell as a way to control moral behavior over the past centuries. Also, I had to admit that, in the matter of suicide, fear of hell probably saved my life. I was very happy that I didn't kill myself.

I enjoyed some of my high school classes; however, I'd picked up bad study habits. I had a good memory and learned to study for tests, on which I usually did well. But I didn't study to really learn and master a subject. This study habit would cause problems later in my ongoing education.

By the time I got toward the end of Algebra 2 I had forgotten the basics from the first year and was having trouble. My problem with Latin was even worse. Despite four years of Latin classes, this dead language remained a major source of confusion for me. I got by somehow, but had not learned the basics and knew that I would pay for it later.

In terms of socialization with my peers I had mixed results. I had never been one of the popular kids in class. I didn't expect to be and it didn't bother me. But I had several close friends and never felt excluded. Jim Ogurchock was my closest friend. I had known Jim all through grammar school. He had two older sisters who were both in the same convent that my sister Roseanna had entered, as well as an older brother, John, who was studying to be a Maryknoll priest. Maryknoll became my choice of where to study for the priesthood too.

Jim and I used to talk about the future and what we'd do when we graduated. He also became a priest and first joined the Glenmary Fathers, a mission group dedicated to helping the American poor. He later left that order, transferred to the diocese of Columbus, Ohio, and remained a priest.

John, his older brother, remained a Maryknoll priest and worked in a jungle parish on a Bolivian river that eventually fed into the Amazon. The Ogurchock sisters remained in the convent. John has since died, as have his two sisters.

My high school graduation picture, June 1950

Although my high school was co-educational, I did not make friends with any of the girls. I didn't consider myself to be attractive and felt clumsy and tongue-tied with girls. I just didn't know how to talk with them. I had no trouble getting through the normal school activities, but that was it.

I attended some dances with Jim and our mutual cousin, Dot Rauckhorst, who was two years ahead of us in school. She was an enthusiastic person and fun to be with. But I didn't know how to dance and spent those evenings conversing with male friends and hanging out on the sidelines.

By my senior year, I just wanted to graduate and move on with my life. I applied to the Maryknoll Foreign Mission Society and was accepted as a seminarian.

THE VENARD SUMMER SCHOOL

In June 1950, shortly after graduating from high school, I was assigned to summer school at The Venard, a Maryknoll junior seminary (or high school) near Scranton, Pennsylvania for six weeks of Latin studies. This was the start of nine years of seminary training.

On our first night at The Venard my fellow students and I heard the rector announce the beginning of military action in Korea. The North Korean communists had attacked Seoul, South Korea and the United States had responded with a military police action. This was the beginning of my education in world politics.

I don't think I had ever even heard of Korea. Until then I had no interest in politics, either American or global. In my very black and white world, Democrats were good and Republicans were not. And during World War II, I had considered Germany and Japan to be evil, particularly Hitler and Tojo. In my mind, it was now the godless North Korean communists who were bad.

Maryknoll had priests assigned to missionary work in South Korea and we knew that the Korean War would affect them and the Catholic Church there. In fact, several Maryknoll priests were imprisoned. We prayed for the Maryknollers in Korea and were informed about the situation from time to time. But our main focus was on our studies. We never read newspapers or watched television. The Korean war and national politics didn't really affect our everyday lives.

I enjoyed The Venard summer school where I met students from all over the United States, including several older men who had been in the army. Hearing tales about their military experiences was an education in itself. During my nine years of seminary training many men came and went. A few stayed in touch after they left, but most did not. Some men from that first summer class persevered and went on to ordination. Several were classmates of mine.

I spent every morning in Latin class that summer. Unfortunately, my old, ineffective study habits persisted. I got by that summer, but didn't really learn any Latin. Afternoons were spent performing manual labor (including working on the farm) and then participating in recreational activities like swimming, playing ball, and hiking. I enjoyed the fact that there was always something to do.

LAKEWOOD JUNIOR COLLEGE

I was then assigned to Maryknoll's junior seminary in Lakewood, New Jersey. The school campus had been a naval training center during World War II. Maryknoll bought the property and opened the school to manage the influx of seminarians they experienced after the war.

The freshmen slept in the barracks while the sophomores got to share a room in the permanent housing unit. Another building housed the faculty and administration. Best of all, there was a gym and recreation building alongside a large playing field big enough for four softball games played simultaneously. The whole campus had been built in the middle of a pine forest and there were huge pine trees scattered throughout it.

In the 1950s Lakewood was known as a resort town that catered to Jewish people. The story was told that Lakewood's major hotel had been exclusive and discriminated against any Jewish clientele. One day a Jewish man (Nathan Straus, the co-owner of Macy's department stores) arrived and was refused a room. Greatly incensed, he bought the property next door, built his own hotel, and opened it up to the Jewish population.

Life in the junior seminary was controlled by bells. Every minute of every day was assigned an activity and every activity was announced by a bell. A bell woke you at 6:30 a.m. We had twenty minutes before the next bell when we were expected to be in church for morning prayers, meditation, and Mass.

The next bell was for breakfast, followed by another bell for twenty minutes of morning duties. We were all assigned to some housecleaning chore, such as sweeping stairs or cleaning classrooms and restrooms. The bell ending that activity gave us twenty minutes to make our beds and be in the classroom.

The rest of the morning was spent in classes, followed by lunch, followed by one hour of manual labor, followed by one hour of recreation, followed by twenty minutes to shower and get to class or study until dinner time. After dinner, we had a recreation period, said the rosary in groups of three outdoors, and then attended study hall. Finally, we said night prayers and were off to bed.

Being slow-moving by nature, responding to these bells was initially a problem for me. If we were late for anything we were expected to report to the dean of discipline after dinner. At first, I was in that line practically every night. As the year went on, I got better at it. But that first year it was truly embarrassing!

Besides reporting being late, we were expected to report any infraction of the rules, such as breaking silence periods by talking, staying up late, or missing any activity. The "great silence" extended from night prayers until breakfast the following morning.

Not surprisingly, my biggest academic problem was Latin. I was not doing well in Latin class. Shortly before the Christmas break, I was called down to see the rector. He told me that the faculty had voted to expel me by a vote of 5 or 6 to 1; however, I was being given one more chance to do better.

I remember walking out of the meeting in shock thinking, *I've got to do better. If I get kicked out, I won't be able to keep my vow to God to become a priest and I will be doomed to hell.* I was scared because I wasn't sure I could do better in Latin. I tried harder, but still wasn't making much progress.

Halfway through the second semester the academic dean, not the rector, called me in. He noted how well I was doing in chemistry. That felt good. I was finally getting credit for doing well in something. But the dean then noted that I still wasn't doing well in Latin. He told me that the faculty thought I must be spending too much time on chemistry. They decided that I should drop chemistry so as to leave more time for me to study Latin.

All I could say was "Yes, Father," but I was crushed. Chemistry was the one subject I was doing well in and now I had to drop it. I didn't think I was studying chemistry too much. All I had to do was memorize a few formulas. That was easy for me compared to Latin.

After this I did spend more time studying Latin, but it didn't help much. Study time was not the problem—basic confusion was, and my study approach didn't do anything to help dispel that confusion. I had never learned to understand the grammatical vocabulary. For example, I never knew what pluperfect meant.

In the final Latin class of the semester, I received my test results. The professor had averaged up all the scores and I ended up with 60, the lowest passing grade. What a relief! But upon taking a second look, I realized he had recalculated that grade and changed it to 59.66.

I had failed by one-third of a point! I couldn't believe it. That really hurt. The joke was on me. But, to my great relief, there wasn't any more talk of expelling me. I would just have to attend summer school at The Venard again. That summer school was a pleasant repeat of the previous summer and this time I did pass my Latin classes.

Once a month at Lakewood a movie was rented for our entertainment. A faculty member was responsible for selecting the movie to make sure it was appropriate for our viewing. We never knew ahead of time which Saturday would be selected for that month's movie, but we soon learned that the truck delivering the movie would arrive shortly after lights out on Friday evening. Every Friday evening, we would listen for that truck. When it came you could hear a very quiet cheer running through the halls.

One incident at Lakewood was totally unexpected. I was called on for something in class and, after I responded, the teacher lit into me about my "lazy lips." He went on for several minutes talking about students with "lazy lips." I didn't know what he was talking about. Here I was, a sophomore in college, and no one had ever said a word to me about poor diction.

Neither my parents, my siblings, my friends, my grammar school and high school teachers nor my classmates had ever told me that I had "lazy lips" or gave me any indication that I had a speech impediment of any kind. This criticism came to me out of the blue! Not knowing what he was talking about, I went on as before. No one followed up to explain what he meant, or even to confirm that I had a diction problem. And I was too introverted to ask anyone about it.

My second year at Lakewood was much better because the Latin studies were actually easier. I still didn't excel, but neither did I flirt with flunking the subject. I did well in the other subjects as well and, by the end of the second semester, I had brought my class rank way up. And I was promoted to the junior class at the Maryknoll College located in Glen Ellyn, Illinois.

MARYKNOLL COLLEGE IN GLEN ELLYN

A few months after arriving at Maryknoll College in Glen Ellyn, I was informed that I was to accompany two other seminarians to Chicago to see a speech therapist. I was both surprised and puzzled. I figured I must have a problem, but I certainly didn't know what it was.

During the years of seminary training, if you were sent, you went. I don't remember where we went or the name of the middle-aged, female speech therapist with whom appointments had been made for the three of us. She started with the oldest student who said his problem was "blocking." That was when I learned that "blocking" was the preferred term for stuttering. I forget why the second student was there.

Finally, she turned to me and asked why I was there. I didn't know, but didn't want to sound ignorant so I said something which I no longer remember. She then asked me to say the word "closed." I said it. She said "No," repeated the word very distinctly, and asked me to say it again. I did, but the result was the same. She then told me that I was not pronouncing the final consonant sounds of some words, such as the final "t" and "d" sounds.

She kept working with me until I finally heard the difference. Finally, she told me it was up to me to practice enunciating final consonants and that was it. I was amazed. I was twenty-one years old and no one but that teacher at The Venard had ever previously intimated that I had a speech impediment. In one 15-minute session, this speech therapist identified the problem and helped me hear it. Now that I could hear it, I could start to remediate the problem.

Back at Lakewood we had a half-hour of free time after dinner. So, I would search out an empty classroom and practice enunciating those final consonants. I quickly learned that, if I concentrated, I could read distinctly and correctly. Many years later, however, I could still find myself slipping back into that "lazy lips" habit in casual conversation.

During those practice sessions long ago, I wondered why I never learned to talk clearly like everyone else . . . naturally. And I've often wondered why it took twenty-one years to find out that I had this problem.

Now, you can probably guess what an interesting singer I was! I couldn't hear whether or not I was on key, so I learned to sing silently. A grade school teacher once told me to silently "just move my lips" while singing with my classmates. My family laughed whenever I attempted the simplest tunes, like the "Happy Birthday" song. I felt deprived of the great joy of song and determined that, if I had to come back in another life, I wanted to be able to sing well. My wife would also add that I be able to dance well too!

In 1952 Maryknoll College in Glen Ellyn was fairly new and Maryknoll had had to double the number of buildings on campus to handle the influx of seminarians during those years. Why such an increase of men seeking to enter religious life and prepare for the priesthood? My less-than-expert opinion identified several factors. The experience of World War II and the threat of extinction represented by the atomic bomb made many people think more seriously about the spiritual meaning of life. Thomas Merton's autobiography, *Seven Story Mountain,* also inspired many young people to consider religious life.

The Catholic culture of the times was also a strong contributing factor. Catholic lives were centered on the local parish church and school where diocesan priests and members of religious orders (priests, brothers, and nuns) were always a major presence. Their lives and teachings exerted a constant influence on the life and religious practice of every Roman Catholic.

In 1960 Pope John XXIII made the momentous announcement that he was calling for a Second Vatican Council. He is said to have stated that, in doing so, he wanted to throw open the windows of the Roman Catholic Church and let fresh air in. He also urged Catholics to emerge from their Catholic ghettos and engage with the world. How the documents of Vatican II changed everything for me is discussed later in this book.

The Glen Ellyn campus was built in the middle of a golf course, leaving nine holes intact on the surrounding grounds. It was claimed that Al Capone used to play golf there. Students with golfing experience loved it, but I learned how terrible one can be at the sport. I loved playing sports and considered myself at least average, although never good enough to make any varsity team.

I tried golf, but all I accomplished was embarrassing myself and frustrating my fellow students who just wanted to play a round. I couldn't hit the ball with a driver. I tried again and again, but I couldn't do it. When we went on to irons, I did okay. I didn't really try putting because I was too discouraged by then.

In later years, I tried golf again and still couldn't do well because I wasn't able to hold my head straight. I'd look up before the club ever came down. In golf, I was still headed in the wrong direction.

Being a junior at Glen Ellyn was exhilarating for me. The Latin classes were over and I could move on to studying other subjects that I might enjoy a lot more. Seminarians were not given a choice about what classes to take. Philosophy was our major field of study. I didn't mind that, but what I did mind was the Vatican decreeing that philosophy and theology books in seminaries were to be in Latin.

Although Latin was categorized as a dead language, it was still the universal language of the Roman Catholic Church. For those proficient in learning languages studying books written in Latin was not a problem, but I would have learned a lot more if the books had been in English.

Our philosophy books were based on the works of Saint Thomas Aquinas and I liked that. I remembered one of our professors warning us to "Beware the man of one book." But we weren't encouraged to read other works and I really didn't have time to do so.

I only remembered taking one elective during my time at Glen Ellyn—a course about English Catholic novelists, such as Evelyn Waugh. Reading any kind of English literature was my favorite hobby.

I did well in my studies at Glen Ellyn. I didn't excel as a very top student, but I no longer had any problem learning the subjects. I even stopped worrying about getting good grades and just enjoyed the classes, knowing my grades would be okay. That didn't mean I didn't have to study. I always felt I had more to learn and that it was important that I do so.

Later, while studying theology at Maryknoll's major seminary in Ossining, New York my classmates, Ben Zweber and Milt Rosera, chided me about studying too much. The Maryknoll major seminary campus included a farm run by the Maryknoll brothers. Ben and Milt had grown up on farms and liked to help out on this farm, but I rarely did. They told me that Brother Rene wanted to know why I had changed.

During one of the two summers I spent at The Venard, I had volunteered on Saturday afternoons to help Brother Rene with his farm work. The implication was that, now that I was at the major seminary studying theology, I felt doing farm work was beneath me. Actually, I would have preferred to be out working on the farm.

THE MARYKNOLL NOVITIATE

In 1954 I graduated from Maryknoll College in Glen Ellyn with a BA degree in Philosophy. My class-mates and I then entered the Maryknoll novitiate located in Bedford, Massachusetts for a year of study concerning spirituality, so as to to further develop our spiritual lives. It was also a "weeding out" year. All through seminary training there was always a steady trickle of guys leaving.

At Lakewood one year a car drove up and a poten-tial student got out. He looked around, got back into the car, and left. Most students gave it a better try. However, as the novitiate year went on our class kept getting smaller and smaller. Someone left on almost a weekly basis. It was just part of our lives.

Whenever we heard that someone was called down to the rector's office, it usually meant he was on his way out. He may have gotten expelled, like I nearly did. However, I think that most of those leav-ing decided on their own that this was not the life for them. Every time students went home for Christmas and summer breaks, some did not return.

In the novitiate, the decision about whether to stay or leave became more serious. This was the time to focus on our spirituality and vocation and whether we were going to commit ourselves to the life of a celibate missionary priest. At the end of the novitiate year, we would take an oath to Maryknoll and become official members of The Foreign Mission Society of America (also known as Maryknoll).

Before this happened, our superiors had to decide if they thought we measured up. Because Maryknoll is a foreign missionary society, a seminarian's health status was especially important. In the mid-1950s, Maryknollers were assigned to missionary work in other countries for a period of ten years, often in regions with few or no health care facilities.

The increased convenience of transportation via jet airplanes led to the assignment time being lowered to six years, and then to three years for my second assignment. French missionary priests in South Korea at the time considered their assignments to be permanent and considered it a sign of weakness to ever have to return to France. They expected to die in Korea.

Each of us had to undergo a complete physical exam during the novitiate year. Minor health problems had to be remedied before we advanced to the major seminary. Some novices were asked to leave on the basis of fairly minor health problems. A heart murmur was a serious disqualification. To my surprise, some of my classmates were sent for psychiatric consults. A couple of them, whom I especially respected, explained to me that they were leaving on the psychiatrist's recommendation.

It was sad to see so many of my classmates leave, but I never considered this being an option for me. And, as far as I knew, our Maryknoll superiors and spiritual directors never concluded that I should leave.

However, I did have to undergo a tonsillectomy, which required a three or four day stay at the Bon

Secour Hospital in Lawrence, Massachusetts. It was my first surgery and I was totally unprepared to wake up with a terribly painful hole in my throat.

After being cared for so well at the hospital, it was quite a shock to return to the novitiate. It was then that I realized how spartan and demanding our life in the novitiate was and would later be on the missions. After my tonsillectomy I was expected to fall right back into the regular novitiate routine. I received no special treatment. No one asked whether I was fully recovered or showed any concern for what I'd just been through. I had to ignore my still painful throat and just fall into line. A few days later the pain was gone and I was back in the swing of the schedule, no longer aware of how hard we had it.

How relative and subjective my perceptions of how hard my life in the novitiate was should be mentioned. The fighting in Korea had ended. A couple of my classmates had fought in Korea and told me about how hard that experience was. Our oldest classmate, Leo Decman, had fought in World War II. Many of the students who left us were drafted into military service. I have no doubt that some ended up in jobs that were either physically and/or mentally difficult.

There were periods in my life when I endured either physical or emotional pain that was excruciating, but I doubted that I had suffered as much as many others have in their lives. I was always grateful that I had the strength of my faith to bolster me during those times.

Incidentally, one of our so-called "hardships" during our time in the novitiate was the fact that we were not allowed to see any movies that entire year. This being his first year as novice-master, Father Van Den Bogaard had banned all movies. This was contrary to the custom that had been enjoyed by the novices in previous years. In fact, newly-ordained Maryknoll priests from the local Boston area used to drop by with a movie for the novices to see from time to time.

We, of course, thought that being denied the pleasure of seeing movies was an unlucky break for us. But we really didn't miss seeing movies very much because we were kept busy with prayer, study, manual labor, and other activities. I had to do a lot of house-painting that year but, fortunately, I missed being assigned to help with the turkey slaughters at Thanksgiving and Christmas. Some "not-so-lucky" guys were sent over to a neighboring farm to help out at those times.

All through our college days at Glen Ellyn we had had to take turns reading to the community over the loudspeaker during certain lunch or dinner times. The readings varied. For example, we read about the lives of missionaries in Alaska, about the life of St. Therese of Lisieux, and the book *Kon Tiki*. The worst reading selection was Thomas à Kempis' *The Imitation of Christ* which advised that "Whenever I go into the world, I come back less a man."

We had lived through speech classes every semester at Glen Ellyn, but in the novitiate the emphasis on public speaking was turned up a notch. Each of us was assigned to prepare and give a sermon. Every Friday at dinnertime a student took his turn and delivered his first ever sermon over the loudspeaker to the whole community. Our sermons were supposed to be about ten minutes long, but maybe they just seemed to be that long.

Since we were assigned the date to deliver our sermon alphabetically, we knew months in advance when each one's turn to deliver his sermon would come. This was not helpful because it felt like the proverbial sword of Damocles was hanging over our heads. As one classmate described it: "There you were, calmly going about your business when you suddenly heard the word 'sermon.' At that moment, your stomach flipped and you felt as if you were falling off a cliff."

None of us had ever delivered a sermon before. I certainly didn't feel qualified to do so. What did I know that qualified me to get up before the whole community and deliver a sermon? Still, I was to get up and present a discourse on spirituality or theology or morality. It frightened me to the core.

I eventually delivered that first sermon, just like everyone else, but I don't remember anything about what I said. At a Maryknoll class reunion, a classmate told me he remembered that I kept repeating the same word or phrase. But I had no recollection of this.

I had had some scary moments in speech classes, but I think that first sermon in the novitiate was the scariest sermon or public speech that I ever gave. Delivering sermons after I was ordained couldn't compare. Later, when I was advising students at the University of Wisconsin-Oshkosh, I could empathize with the students who would do anything to avoid a speech class.

MARYKNOLL MAJOR SEMINARY

At the end of the novitiate year, we moved on to the major seminary at Maryknoll's headquarters in Ossining, New York to study theology for four years. After three years of study, we were ordained deacons. And at the end of the fourth year, we were ordained priests and immediately assigned to work in a foreign country.

During those four years we lost a few more classmates. In most cases, the men left silently and we only knew they had departed by their absence. Our class was the largest Maryknoll had ever had and we thought that 59 of us would be ordained. But shortly before ordination we lost two more classmates. Only 57 were ordained in 1959.

Once ordained, did anyone leave? To my knowledge, no one did in the 1950s. In those days priests, for the most part, remained priests no matter what their circumstances. Even priests who reached retirement age and retired continued helping out on weekends in some of the local parishes.

At the novitiate, there had been a couple of older priests who were considered "retired." These men were different from the priests who really retired due to age. No one explained why these older priests were there and we just accepted their presence. The rumor was that one had an alcohol problem. There had also been a Maryknoll brother living at the novitiate who was obviously mentally disturbed and even a little scary. We avoided him as much as we could.

Since our major seminary was located in the Maryknoll headquarters, all the Maryknoll priests passed through at one time or another. Occasionally a priest would stay for a while and be assigned to some work: for example, in the magazine department. The seminarians referred to this work as "licking envelopes," since it was obviously a penitential assignment until the priest straightened out enough to be reassigned to the missions. In most cases, no one ever explained to us seminarians why the penance was necessary.

One of the most painful instances of this situation occurred when a man who had been ordained just the year before showed up. He sat with the other priests in the refectory for meals. All of us knew him but he never looked at us or acknowledged us. He remained very quiet, stayed by himself, kept his head down, and appeared to be deep in shame.

The rumor among us seminarians was that he had slept with a woman on his mission and had to be sent home. To both avoid scandal and change the situation, any priest so involved would be sent back to the States immediately. After doing some penance, this priest was reassigned to another mission. I don't know if he received professional therapy like some priests in a similar situation did.

It was only in the late 1960s and 1970s that many priests who fell in love began to decide to leave the active priesthood and marry, since the Vatican continued to refuse to consider a married priesthood. These men considered marriage to be as sacred a vocation as the priesthood. They didn't really want to leave and many continued to exercise their priestly ministry (unofficially) by presiding at marriages and funerals. I knew of a couple of men who continued functioning as active priests even though they had secret relationships. But eventually they, too, left the priesthood and married the women involved.

Before the mid-1970s a priest could ask to be laicized (withdrawn from clerical status) and, in most cases, the Vatican allowed this. These men left in good standing with the Church. However, under Pope John Paul II (1975-2005), most requests for laicization were denied. This didn't stop priests from leaving the active priesthood. Many of them decided they didn't want to be laicized. They considered themselves to still be priests, even though they had married.

Despite all the problems resulting from the worldwide priest shortage, the Vatican still insists on maintaining a celibate male clergy. The Church's relations with married priests are basically non-existent The Vatican ignores them as if they don't exist. It always seemed hypocritical to me that exceptions were made for Episcopal and Anglican married clergy who wished to become Roman Catholic priests. From my perspective, the sad part was that many of these Protestant clergy were very conservative and converted to Roman Catholicism as their way to express opposition to the acceptance of women priests in their former church affiliations.

But I have digressed. My life studying theology at Maryknoll's major seminary was exciting. Writing assignments, however, tended to be stressful for me. I didn't learn to express my thoughts in writing with ease until years after my ordination to the priesthood—not until I began to get in touch with my feelings with the help of a Jungian psychiatrist.

I enjoyed the communal life and always felt that most of my classmates and the men in the other classes were exceptional people. All of us were dedicated to becoming priests and going forth to do good work for God in the world.

I really wanted to learn theology. At this point in my life, I was still a very obedient man who didn't question authority. In dogmatic theology, I just wanted to learn what the Church taught. Our dogmatic theology classes focused on identifying "proofs" from scripture and tradition. Added to that was the level of belief one was taught to attribute to each dogma. For example, on the highest level of belief the doctrines of the Immaculate Conception and the Assumption of Mary are the only ones declared infallible. On the next level are the doctrines found in the Nicene Creed. On a lower level are doctrines that can be considered controversial and open to discussion.

The overriding principle is the primacy of the individual conscience. The ordination of women to the priesthood continues to be a subject of much controversy. Pope John Paul II declared that women cannot be ordained. Some Vatican authorities believed that this was an infallible statement. However, most theologians today do not believe that this declaration meets the criteria for an infallible declaration and that, therefore, this pronouncement can be questioned.

I didn't give too much attention to those different levels of belief. After all, I believed them all, so what did it matter? Later, though, when I began to question church teachings, these levels of belief still didn't make much sense to me. It seemed to me that you either believed or didn't believe no matter what level of belief was assigned by the Vatican. I didn't dismiss theological dogma since it is meant to help us understand what we believe. But, to me, one's personal relationship with God, and what one understands from that, seemed far more important.

The study of moral theology was different. I grew up thinking everything was either black or white, good or bad. The study of behavior and what made for good moral or immoral decisions was terribly important to me. I learned that moral decisions are never just black or white. In studying actual cases (in their concrete circumstances, not just in the abstract) it can be very difficult to distinguish between moral and immoral decisions. From a pastoral viewpoint, it is necessary to temper judgments about those decisions with compassion and love. Learning this wasn't easy for someone with a background like mine.

Then there was the canon law course where we studied the laws of the Roman Catholic Church. Many of these laws were concerned with the valid administration of the sacraments: for example, what constitutes a valid Mass or baptism or marriage.

Every so often our canon law professor would come in with a story about what a particular missioner had written to him, describing some outrageous administration of a sacrament. For example, a missioner would describe using something like banana oil to baptize someone because there was no available water, or some other obviously invalid behavior.

Our professor would get very incensed about the situation and go on for some time, insisting he had taught that man the correct procedure and warning us about listening carefully and learning in class. He never seemed to catch on that the missioner had written a phony tale, knowing it would upset the professor and earn us a lecture warning. There were occasions, though, when the tales were true and he had every right to be upset.

Certain guys seemed to be especially adept at creating situations or working out jokes that kept the laughter flowing. One of the more clever seminarians, I thought, was the deacon who wanted to go down to New York City. We were granted a "New York Day" only two or three times a year. Outside of that, you had to have a very good reason for going there, usually a medical appointment or family emergency which had to be approved by the rector.

This particular deacon didn't have a legitimate reason for his request, but he still wanted to go down to New York City. So, he approached the rector and asked if he could have a house car to drive there. The rector indignantly told him he should take the train like everybody else. He took that for his permission and off he went to the Big Apple on the train.

CHAPTER 3

Early Missionary Life in Korea

I WAS ORDAINED ON JUNE 13, 1959 AND assigned to South Korea with eight other classmates, one priest ordained a few years earlier, and one brother. Brothers are men who do not wish to become priests but join Maryknoll in order to live a religious life and work on the missions.

Very often brothers are skilled in a trade. One brother in South Korea when I was there was a nurse. Another brother supervised major church construction.

My family attended my first Mass

It was August before transportation was arranged on a merchant ship. Until then, I relaxed at home in Akron with my family. The trip took over two weeks because the ship stopped in Taiwan, Okinawa, and Japan before arriving in Inchon, South Korea. Except for bouts of seasickness, the trip was enjoyable. I read, played games with my classmates, played poker with the crew, and enjoyed visiting cities with Maryknoll missions in Japan and Taiwan.

Upon arriving in South Korea, we were immediately driven to the Maryknoll Center House in Seoul and began eight months of language study. In many ways, it felt like an extension of our studies at the Maryknoll major seminary back home, except that we were studying the Korean language and were surrounded by rice paddies.

In 1959 the Maryknoll Center House was in the countryside outside of Seoul, about a 30-35 minute ride into the city. We had to walk a mile to reach a bus stop if we needed to go into the city.

When I returned for a visit in 1989, Seoul's urban sprawl had surrounded the Maryknoll Center House and advanced miles beyond it. The rice paddies around the Center House were long gone.

I mention the rice paddies because they provided an immediate and odiferous initiation to country life in South Korea. The paddies were fertilized with human excrement. Before the excrement was spread, it was deposited in small pools. On certain days when the pools got stirred up, the smell crept through the windows and doors, adhered to the walls and ceilings, and hung in the air. It was the worst olfactory experience of my whole life.

On the positive side, we could look out the back of the Center House building and see the three famous mountain peaks that rose up just north of the city. In the early 1960s they were always visible. One day Father Ben Zweber and I hiked over to and attempted to climb them. It took us three hours to arrive at a ridge between two of the peaks and I was exhausted. I had to stop and recover while Father Ben climbed to the top of one of the peaks. He came back exhausted and related that he had met a Korean woman coming down the mountain with a load of wood on her head. We were both breathless, but she was not.

When I visited South Korea in 1989, those spectacular mountain peaks were no longer visible. They were obscured by pollution exhaust from the many vehicles that then choked the streets of Seoul. The oxcarts were gone. South Korea had gone modern. However, one evening it rained, cleansing the air of the pollution. The next morning, to my joy, I was able to view the mountains. A few hours later they vanished again. For me, those mountains provided the most spectacular view in Seoul.

LANGUAGE SCHOOL

For Americans, Korean is one of the most difficult languages in the world to learn. The language has sounds that we don't make in English. Some of the sounds are very similar and hard to distinguish from one another. For example, the Korean language has two "p" and two "s" sounds.

As I mentioned before, Maryknollers who had good ears for music learned Korean much more easily than guys like me. I struggled. Some Maryknollers learned the language so quickly, and spoke Korean so well, that Koreans who heard them didn't realize they were not Koreans unless they looked directly at the speaker.

In language school we had class all morning taught by a Korean woman who was a very good teacher. We dubbed her the "Lady Dragon." In the afternoon we studied and practiced speaking Korean with the help of Korean tutors. On weekends we went into the city of Seoul to visit the famous palaces, temples, and other landmarks. Or we would go shopping and wander around, marveling at the crowds, the unceasing movement, and the activity of the sellers, buyers, and workers. This provided a good opportunity to try out our language skills.

I remembered being by myself in the middle of the city early on, waiting for a bus. I had to depend on the bus number to get on the right bus since I hadn't learned enough Korean yet to read the signs. This was scary because, if I couldn't find the right bus, I would be utterly lost without even enough fluency in Korean to ask directions or seek help.

Weekends were also a time to help out. We took turns saying Mass at an American army camp that was about two miles away from the Maryknoll Center House. We also occasionally helped out at a Korean Catholic Center in Seoul. We could say Mass, but none of us were proficient enough to give a sermon in Korean. The people certainly didn't complain about that.

At Christmas and Easter we were sent out to mission parishes to help out. Maryknoll worked in two dioceses under Maryknoll bishops, one in Inchon and one in Chong Ju. Except for the islands off the coast in the Yellow Sea, the Inchon diocese was really an urban setting. Maryknoll also worked in a couple of parishes in Pusan under a Korean Bishop. Chong Ju province was the only land-locked province in South Korea. And, unlike Seoul, Chong Ju was rural and the people there were bound by traditional values and customs.

For my first Christmas in South Korea, I was sent to the city of Chong Ju along with three or four other classmates. The train station was an hour away from our Center House. A two-to-three hour train ride was followed by a bus ride to Chong Ju city. We spent the night there at Bishop Pardy's residence. The next day I traveled by bus by myself to the Chin Chon parish to which I would later be assigned. This part of the trip was anxiety-provoking because, every time the bus stopped, I wondered if this was where I should get off.

The pastor, Father Bill Ahearn, welcomed me to Chin Chon. The day after my arrival was Christmas Eve. We had a late evening candlelight parade through the market town and then Midnight Mass. The church was unheated and December in South Korea is as cold as in New York or Ohio. However, the church was packed that night so it was quite comfortable.

After Christmas day, I developed a pain in my side which gradually got worse. Father Bill drove me in his Jeep, an hour or more away, to a neighboring parish where the Maryknoll sisters had a clinic staffed by a doctor and nurses. The doctor diagnosed a urinary tract infection, gave me an antibiotic, and I recovered quickly.

The Maryknoll sisters' clinic was a tremendous help to our work. Just knowing they were there to attend to any emergency provided a sense of security. There were very few Korean doctors in the Chong Ju province and none at all in the small rural towns where Maryknoll missioners were stationed. In addition to the clinic where we could send emergency patients, the sisters also had a traveling medical van. They visited each rural parish in the surrounding area once a month. People would come from miles around and form a long line, hoping to be seen by the sister doctor.

The sisters warned us about the problem Koreans had adhering to prescribed medicine dosages. For example, they would tell a patient to take a pill every four hours. But, if the pill seemed to be working, the patient would figure that taking two pills would be better than one, and so on.

The catechist in Chin Chon told me about a man who lived just outside the church gate. He was not a Catholic and I never met him. During one of the medical van visits, the doctor gave him some medicine for a cold and cough. He liked the cough syrup so much that he proceeded to drink the whole bottle at one time. The catechist explained that, as a result, the man's throat was paralyzed and he lost his voice.

I was ready to panic, thinking we were in major trouble, about to be blamed for the man's condition. The catechist then reported that the man wasn't angry with us. He just wanted to know if he could get some more of that fantastic syrup. When I related this to the doctor, she told me that the syrup contained a good amount of alcohol.

After my first Korean Christmas in Chin Chon, I traveled in reverse and arrived back at the Center House in Seoul by New Year's Eve. All my classmates and I shared stories about our exciting first adventures in the mission parishes.

I didn't remember a lot of detail about that first trip to Chin Chon. But I did recall how strange and different everything was. Chin Chon seemed to be at the end of the world. Later, when I lived there, I discovered it was not at the end of the world; however, some of the mission stations farther out in the country really were.

Perhaps the most memorable event during that trip was the walk with my classmates from the bus station in Chong Ju to Bishop Pardy's house just before Christmas. It was nighttime and snowing lightly so everything was white—the road, the strangely-built houses, and us. There was no traffic and no other people were on the road so it was unexpectedly quiet. We were walking through the silent whiteness in a strange place where I had never been before, going to an unseen destination. It was beautiful.

I have been asked, "What was the effect of the war on Korea?" I never saw any physical effects of the war like bombed-out buildings. One of my colleagues who had been a soldier in Seoul during the Korean war was amazed at the changes that had taken place just a couple of years after the war. He no longer recognized Seoul.

The war was still very much a part of the Korean people's awareness. Many had personally suffered from it. There were many separated families. Some North Korean family members had escaped to the South, leaving other family members in the North. In most cases, they never heard from each other again. The search for spies was constant. It was said that the president of South Korea, Syngman Rhee, wanted to attack the North and continue the war. The United States army prevented this by very carefully rationing the gas provided to the South Korean army.

The Korean people themselves seemed very open to foreigners, and to Americans in particular. They were very grateful that Americans had fought on their side during the Korean war and helped to preserve their freedom. They didn't necessarily like everything the United States army and its soldiers did, but they recognized how important the presence of the American soldiers was to their safety and security.

Despite their Buddhist traditions, Koreans were very open to Christianity. I think this was partly due to how the relief goods were distributed during and after the war. The relief goods were often distributed by Christian churches. This helped the Christian population continue to grow. Many of the Christian churches in South Korea now focus more on respecting and understanding the Korean Buddhist traditions than on proselytizing the people.

Another question I had been asked was: "How did the people respond to foreign priests like me wandering around wearing a Roman collar?" During the ten years I was in South Korea, I wasn't aware of experiencing any discrimination. But some Koreans who saw me or other priests from afar probably thought we were pretty weird.

For my first Easter in South Korea, I was sent to a parish in Mou Ki, a town much closer to Seoul than Chin Chon where I had spent Christmas. It was also in the diocese of Chong Ju and travel there from Seoul involved a two-hour bus ride directly south.

In those days, buses in South Korea consisted of truck beds that had a bus body built on top of them. The passenger area was less than six feet high. At a little over six feet, I had to stand with my head bowed and pressed against the ceiling. There were seats, but never enough. There were always more people standing than sitting and no one was ever turned away. No matter how full the bus was the drivers would always jam in whoever else might be waiting alongside the road.

The buses were unheated, of course, and the dirt roads were rocky and bumpy. I always marveled at the Koreans' ingenuity and sheer determination to keep those buses running. They didn't have anti-freeze and at night the engine would freeze in wintertime. So, the workers would build a fire underneath the engine to melt the frozen oil and enable them to start the bus in the morning. Many times I saw workers using their bare hands to work with the metal parts in freezing weather to complete a repair.

I didn't recall there being a lot of accidents but there must have been some. The only time I was ever frightened was one evening, when the driver was in a hurry and seemed to be speeding along on an especially bumpy roadway. Suddenly the bus lurched and I quickly lodged myself in behind a seat. Looking out the window, I saw our rear wheel and tire go bouncing by us, eventually rolling into a field. The bus came to a crunching stop and I was grateful that no one was hurt.

Since the early 1960s the Korean diet had improved. As a result, the average height of the population increased. But I didn't remember ever meeting a Korean as tall as I was. In the mid-1960s I was responsible for building a small chapel on one of our mission stations. I had a discussion with the carpenter who argued that the entrance door should only be four feet high. I was incensed. Who put four-foot-high doors on houses or other buildings? He insisted that the people would like it better because this would help lessen heat loss in the winter. Body heat was the only source of heat in the churches during the 1960s. Despite this, I insisted that the doorway had to be high enough for me to walk through it without bowing or bumping my head.

Now, back to my first Easter in South Korea. I rode the bus to Father Ray Oberowsky's Mou Ki parish and participated in all the Easter liturgies. I didn't know it at the time, but Mou Ki would become my first parish as pastor two years later. These parish visits were especially rewarding because you felt you were finally doing what you had come to South Korea to do.

Back at the Maryknoll Center House we resumed our language studies. Besides the Center House being the site for our language school, it was also the residence of the Maryknoll regional superior, the man responsible for all the Maryknollers working in South Korea. Any Maryknoller needing to see the regional superior, and/or needing to come to Seoul for business or for a short break from life in the country, stayed at the Center House.

This was a great plus since we language students were gradually introduced to all the men stationed in South Korea. They numbered about sixty at the time. It was usual for two or more guys at a time to be passing through. In the evening, they would gather around the dining table, drink O'B beer, and tell stories about what was happening in their parishes.

I could no longer recall most of their stories in detail, but still remembered the humor. It was the missioners' way of letting off steam and their stories were very funny. For example, Father Dowd talked about officiating at a marriage in his parish. In the South Korean country towns in those days, marriages were arranged by the parents. The couple might meet briefly prior to the wedding, but they really didn't know each other.

This particular marriage ceremony, and the celebration afterwards, went smoothly and then the couple retired for the night. All hell broke loose during the night when the bride delivered a baby boy. No one on the groom's side knew she was pregnant.

The next morning there was a big argument, with the groom's family insisting that the marriage was off and that the bride was to take her baby boy and go back to her family. Father Dowd argued for preserving the marriage, pointing out that the baby was a boy.

It may be different now, but in those days a marriage—including a Catholic marriage—wasn't necessarily secure until the woman produced a male heir. Father Dowd argued a good point but, not surprisingly, the groom's family still broke up the marriage.

On a similar note, a Catholic man in one of my parishes was devastated because his wife produced seven girls and no boy. Being Catholic, he knew he wasn't allowed to divorce his wife or take a concubine, but there was always tremendous peer pressure to do so.

After we finished language school at the end of May 1960, we had a short vacation during which Fathers Leo Decman, Pat Patterson, and I went to Ulsan. This trip involved a very long train ride to the southeastern coast of South Korea where a French priest had established a convent to train Korean women to become religious sisters. The sisters then worked in various parishes throughout South Korea, including several parishes in the Chong Ju diocese.

During this very relaxing week we swam in the ocean and had our meals outdoors with two French priests, one of whom was in his nineties. He attributed his longevity to taking a cold shower every day.

I was surprised the first morning when we asked for coffee. The waitress, who was a postulant aspiring to become a sister, poured from two pots at the same time, one with coffee and one with milk, giving us half a cup of each. Father Leo explained that this was "café au lait," the French way of serving coffee. Coffee was new to South Korea at that time and most people had never tasted it.

Coffee houses gradually sprang up in Seoul, catering to university students. I ordered black coffee in a coffee house in Seoul one day and the waitress argued that I wouldn't like it without milk and sugar. I insisted on getting black coffee. She delivered the coffee as I requested, but also placed milk and sugar on the table. She was sure I would need it. No matter how bitter, I always preferred unsweetened black coffee.

We had coffee in our rectories, but not on the mission stations. I felt a craving for coffee on trips out to the mission stations and eventually realized this meant I was addicted to caffeine. When I reached my sixties, I developed atrial fibrillation and decided I had better break the coffee habit. It took enduring a week of painful headaches to do so.

CHIN CHON: MY FIRST ASSIGNMENT

After language school, I was assigned by my Maryknoll regional superior to the Chong Ju diocese. Bishop Pardy, the bishop for the Chon Ju diocese, sent me to Chin Chon to be curate, or assistant pastor, at Father Bill Ahearn's parish. By now I could manage some limited conversation in Korean, but I was still struggling with the language. And my Christmas and Easter mission trips during language school had been my only parish experiences.

I figured I should get to Chin Chon a few days early because Father Bill would be leaving for his vacation shortly after my arrival. I needed a few days to at least find out what was expected of me.

This time I took a train halfway to Chong Ju in order to switch to a bus that would take me directly to Chin Chon. Although it was still afternoon, I found that I had missed the last bus to Chin Chon. So, I had to board a later train to Chong Ju and go to the bishop's residence to spend the night there. I arrived in Chin Chon later the next morning.

Father Bill informed me that I had been expected the day before and many of the young parishioners had gathered to welcome me. They were disappointed that I hadn't shown up. But now that I was there, Father Bill could leave for his vacation. He quickly packed his bag, got in his Jeep, and left.

To my plea for some kind of directions, Father Bill replied that I only needed to consult with the catechist if I had any questions. He was right. The catechist took care of the daily issues of running the parish and I attended to the Mass and the sacraments.

I spent nearly a full year in Chin Chon. There weren't a lot of priests in Chong Ju at the time, only an average of one priest per parish. When new priests came, Bishop Pardy would start a new parish. Being one of the few curates in the diocese, I was often sent by the bishop to fill in at other parishes when those priests were due for their vacations. This was great experience for me since I got to know many of the parishes and towns, the catechists, and how different priests managed their parishes.

It wasn't until that Fall in Chin Chon that I was hit by homesickness. It was harvesting time and the farmers were clearing the rice paddies. Only they were no longer rice paddies—they were fields of mud with tied-up bundles of rice stalks standing in the mud. I remembered how the bundles of wheat stood on beautiful fields in the Ohio countryside. This harvest time, along with my struggles with the language, really got me down. How could I understand the Korean culture if I couldn't understand their language and appreciate their customs?

Though I didn't realize it then, I was experiencing Korean culture and customs all the time. Traveling to the mission stations was one example. Throughout the winter, after the harvest, Father Bill tried to visit each of his several mission stations at least once a month. This was a big change from the old tradition when there were very few priests available and mission stations were visited once a year at most. We could drive to some mission stations, but getting to others required a long hike over or around the mountains. If we had to hike in to a mission station, we had to spend the night there.

After arriving at a mission station, we spent hours hearing confessions in the freezing cold little church buildings because everyone at the mission station would want to confess. Then Mass was celebrated, followed by talking with and quizzing new converts preparing for baptism.

After that we ate whatever we were served and spent the evening chatting with everyone. We could always count on being served rice and kim chi. Soup with eggs along with dumplings, seaweed, chicken, and various small vegetable side dishes might also be served.

It was fun to experience what Korean life was like in the 1960s in the Chong Ju "end of the world" countryside. For example, we sat on the traditional Korean ondal floor. The kitchen was at the side of the house and below the level of the house's floor. The heat from the cooking fires circulated through the floor of the house. This was a very efficient way to heat the one or two rooms of the house.

Everyone sat on the ondal floor. And a small foot-high table was used for meals. The woman who served the meal would climb the few steps from the kitchen to the outside, round the corner and climb a couple more steps onto the small porch. Then she would slide open the door and enter the room to serve the food. In summer, the meal could be served on the porch which would be cooler than on the heated floor. The woman had to brave the weather no matter what the season.

The hardest thing on the mission stations for me was using the outhouses. They were often square structures with thick straw walls around a hole covered by some boards with an opening over the hole. There was nothing to sit on. You crouched and, when you were done, you got out of there as fast as you could to avoid being overcome by the smell. I used them only in absolute emergencies.

One mission station trip stood out for me. Father Bill sent me to a mission station without him that involved a hike of about two hours into the mountains. Since it was starting to rain, I questioned the wisdom of such a hike in the rain. Father Bill dismissed the rain and off I went with the catechist and a couple of others to help. He didn't want me to look for an excuse not to go. The visit was scheduled, so I should go.

It rained heavily the whole way. When we arrived, the people were quite surprised to see us. Because of the heavy rain, they hadn't expected us to come and everyone had remained at home. We stayed the night and the next day the rain stopped. The people all came out then and we had our usual visit.

When we got back from this mission station, the catechist explained how badly it had rained and how no one had shown up. Father Bill apologized. I learned from this experience the importance of these visits and how adaptable the Korean people were.

Incidentally, there is no place in South Korea without mountains. If you are traveling, you have to go around them or over them, but you can't avoid them. In the 1960s, going over them could be difficult because of the dirt roads and poor means of transportation. Today, South Korean roads are all paved and transportation is modern. The problem now is the crush of traffic, since the number of vehicles on the roads has increased exponentially.

CHONG HO WON

I had been an assistant pastor for nearly a year at Chin Chon when, in late Spring 1961, I was reassigned to be an assistant pastor in Chong Ho Won. This parish was about 30 miles north of Chin Chon and 50 or 60 miles south of Seoul. I was replacing

Father Al Keene, the current assistant pastor at Chong Ho Won.

Father Keene's new assignment was to be pastor of the Mou Ki parish which was about 10-15 miles south of Chong Ho Won. Father Ray Oberowski, who started the Mou Ki parish, had completed his six-year tour in South Korea and was returning to the States for six months. When he came back to South Korea he would be assigned as pastor at a different parish. The bishop did not believe in anyone being a permanent pastor because, as missioners, we were supposed to be willing to move on. More to the point, as missioners we were ultimately supposed to work ourselves out of our jobs and be replaced by Korean priests.

The Chong Ho Won parish had an interesting history. I remembered it being the oldest church in the region and, at one time, the parish included a large part of the entire province. It had been established by one of the early French missioners in South Korea. He eventually built a rather large church in Chong Ho Won which he had intended to become the bishop's cathedral. Instead, Bishop Pardy built his cathedral in Chong Ju, the capital city of the province.

The Chong Ho Won church and rectory were built partway up the side of a mountain overlooking a large valley. It was very picturesque. I loved the view from the balcony of the French-style rectory which was built of stone with large unheated rooms and high ceilings.

The parish included grammar, middle, and high schools. Father Ryan was the pastor. He had been my history professor for one year back in the States.

Father Craig was also assigned there to be in charge of the schools. He was one of the older Maryknollers who had worked in North Korea before the Korean War.

Part of my job was to teach English in the boys' high school. I had always found teaching classes to be stressful, even in the States. I took the job seriously and tried to teach English conversation. Later, I learned that the students weren't very happy with my approach. They really wanted to learn English, but mainly to understand what they read so they could pass the English test required for entrance into the university.

Another difficulty I encountered in Chong Ho Won was due to my poor understanding of Father Ryan. In the evenings he liked to go into the village in the valley below us and visit with certain families. It enabled him to learn a lot about what was happening among the people in the parish, including all the gossip, scandals, and difficulties the people were experiencing. Sometimes they drank Korean rice wine and he believed he could imbibe without anyone knowing when he'd had too much.

I was with Father Ryan one time when he was obviously inebriated and kept repeating the same thing over and over. The people ignored it. The next day he told me that he had been drunk, but still able to talk as if everything was okay, so no one knew. I didn't have the guts to tell him what I had observed.

I rarely accompanied Father Ryan on these visits. Instead, I stayed in the rectory, studying Korean and preparing for the next day's class. I made sure to be in bed before Father Ryan returned because, If I happened to be up when he returned, he would begin talking and continue for hours. I never saw him sleep; instead, he sat up in his chair all night. Only later did I realize that Father Ryan's drinking and talkativeness late at night were defenses in his attempt to remain a good priest.

Two years after I had moved on to Mou Ki, Father Ryan became the first Maryknoller in South Korea to leave the priesthood. He married a Korean woman from Chong Ho Won and went to work for the English language daily paper in Seoul. He stayed in South Korea several years, but eventually moved back to upstate New York. One motivating factor for his return to the States was the fact that school-age children of mixed-race marriages were the object of discrimination in South Korea.

I always felt ashamed that I wasn't more aware of and understanding about Father Ryan's personal struggles. I certainly had no complaints about his personal relationship with me. And I don't remember him ever saying an unkind word to me or correcting anything that I had done. I'm sure that I must have given him occasion to do so.

As assistant pastor in the parish, I had to carry my share of the workload. Father Ryan did not have a Jeep and he recommended that I obtain a bicycle, since that was how we traveled to the mission stations. The catechist, Mr. Kim, always traveled with us. He was an older man, maybe around fifty, who had a son in the seminary. He was what we called an "Old Catholic."

Old Catholics in South Korea were descendants of the original converts in the 1800s who had survived and persevered as Catholics despite persecutions and martyrdom at certain times. To protect themselves, they retreated into the hills and became pottery makers. Although pottery makers didn't enjoy high status, Old Catholics were thus able to avoid attention while contributing a necessary service to the community.

Usually, every parish had an enclave of these very faithful Old Catholics. New Catholics were those who had been recently baptized, many of them since the end of the Korean War. Catholicism and Christianity were attractive to the Koreans and there was a steady influx of new converts. The New Catholics eventually outnumbered the Old Catholics.

Our Old Catholic catechist, Mr. Kim, was an educated, intelligent man who was respected and appreciated by the people. On the mission stations, he was always welcomed and made the visits especially enjoyable.

One mission station visit was memorable. We had to travel over five miles by bicycle to the first mission station and then hike over a mountain to arrive at the second mission station tucked into a little village behind the mountain.

Maybe because these parishioners were so far out and didn't get many visitors, they always seemed to be extra happy that we had come. Having a Jeep wouldn't have helped us get to this mission station. You had to hike over the mountain.

Father Jimmy Ray, one of our older priests, told about visiting that mission station during his stay in Chong Ho Won. About halfway up the mountain, he needed to sit and rest. Along came an old man who sat down and talked with him a bit. Finally, the old man said he had to go, got up, and climbed the mountain with ease while Father Ray watched with envy.

I was always amazed at how physically fit the people seemed to be. It was not unusual to see 60-year-old men and women come running down the path to catch the bus. I even heard of pregnant women interrupting their work in the fields to deliver their babies.

Father Craig was the third priest at Chong Ho Won. He was an old-timer, who had worked in what is now North Korea before World War II. He was there as the principal of the boys' Catholic high school. Occasionally, I drove with Father Craig in his Jeep to diocesan meetings and the like. He had the reputation of being a bad driver. I quickly learned that he deserved that reputation! Riding the bus was safer, despite the inconvenience it entailed.

Father Craig was the worst driver I had ever ridden with, even worse than my wife's elderly uncle. He would yell at people walking along the road. One time, he came very close to running over a young man who hadn't scattered as fast as the others. If the young man hadn't jumped out of the way quickly enough, he would have been hit. Father Craig stopped and told me to get out and apologize to the people for what he had done. When I did, they merely looked back at me in disbelief.

I was happy that I no longer had any occasion to ride with Father Craig when I moved away from Chong Ho Won. Not surprisingly, he claimed to be a very good driver and thought that he was doing a great favor for anyone who rode with him.

Typical village kids in the church yard

MOU KI

In Spring 1962, I was assigned to the parish of Mou Ki as pastor. Father Al Keene had been assigned to a larger parish which included the Maryknoll sisters' clinic.

Some parishioners in Mou Ki were upset about this reassignment because they liked Father Keene and the parish catechist. Father Keene recommended that I hire a different catechist because the current parish catechist had a drinking problem. One of the leading women in the parish never attended church as long as I was there because of being upset by the departure of both Father Keene and his catechist.

Despite this, being assigned to Mou Ki was probably the best thing that could have happened to me. I was the only one in town who spoke English. To survive I really had to learn conversational Korean. It was total immersion, sink or swim. I finally began to hear and understand the language and to carry on conversations with the people.

Father Al with two boys in their school uniforms

Women in typical 1960s garb

One incident exemplified my ongoing struggles with the Korean language. A catechist from our most distant mission station came in to tell me about a problem. I just couldn't understand him. He wasn't making any sense to me. Finally, after a couple of trips back to my room to consult my Korean-English dictionary, I discovered that he was telling me about someone who had died and was asking about the funeral arrangements. The problem was that the word he used for funerals had two meanings. I knew the first meaning, but not the meaning indicating a funeral.

Father Al with Easter week bridal party at Mou Ki, circa 1964

The bride was just baptized at Easter. Because of the relatively small number of Catholics available and the Korean custom of matching the bride and groom, it was hard to arrange a Catholic marriage, so this was a special event.

Incidentally, my replacement at Chong Ho Won was Father Al Fleming. Years later, I learned that his language tutor was the uncle of the two Korean girls, Ann and Lisa, that Louise and I were to adopt. The girls weren't born until the 1970s, but the family had been living in Chong Ho Won while I was assigned there. The girls' grandparents also had a farm back in the hills behind one of the mission stations of the Mou Ki parish. It was about halfway between Mou Ki and Chin Chon. The girls were familiar with Mou Ki and the small chapel I had built at that mission station.

Although I started out at Mou Ki scared-to-death, I began to enjoy the parish work as I made progress in my language fluency and felt more comfortable conversing in Korean. It turned out that I wasn't as helpless as I thought.

The Mou KI parish was small, with between 500 to 700 parishioners, but it covered a large geographic area. It included eight mission stations, each one between five to ten miles away from the main church. Half of the parishioners lived on the mission stations.

It was quite a job getting to each station once a month, depending on the season. We didn't visit in the early Spring during the planting season or in the Fall during the harvest season. I traveled the dirt roads by bicycle and was always accompanied by the main parish catechist and one or two helpers.

Each mission station had its own catechist who led Sunday services and organized all events. This catechist was chosen by the people themselves. If there was no chapel, we met in his house.

I managed to build chapels in three mission stations while I was there. The people were poor, but they contributed something to the cost. The bishop provided the major funding. These chapels seated around 100 people sitting on the floor and were an important addition to each village since they could also be used as village meeting halls.

Before I arrived in South Korea, Father Joe Herbert had discovered a brick-making machine that compressed the right kind of mud-clay and straw mixture into very solid bricks. On the right foundation, a very strong, stable one-story building could be built. The only caveat was that they needed to be covered with plaster to prevent rain from washing the bricks away. We were able to build these mud-brick chapels for about $2000 each.

One of the brick chapels built on the Mou Ki mission stations

Traveling by bicycle had its difficult moments. On one extremely frustrating trip the frozen ground had melted enough to make the road a quagmire. We could only pedal about 50 feet before the mud would cake under the bike fenders, stopping any progress. We had to stop over and over to clear away the mud. The quagmire extended for some distance and I thought we'd never get to the mission station. On the way home that evening, the road was again frozen and it was smooth going.

Since much of this travel was in the winter, it was usually dark on the way home and, of course, there were no streetlights. We had a light mounted on our handlebars that was lit up by the movement of the pedals. The faster you pedaled, the brighter the light. If you wanted to see where you were going, you had to keep pedaling at a good rate. If you slowed down in order to be careful (for example, when crossing a stream), the light dimmed or even went out altogether.

My first catechist, a college graduate, was an enormous help to me. He was very intelligent and we worked very well together. Being a young man, he had no trouble traveling by bicycle with me. He also had the respect of all the people, which was important. Unfortunately for me, he had come intending to help me out only temporarily. After two years, his wife and father insisted that he return to his home in Chong Ju to help with the family pharmacy business.

Bicycle travel cost me my next catechist. He was a middle-aged man and a very experienced catechist from Chung Ju, the province's second largest city. He was a great asset and I was extremely lucky to be able to hire him to come to Mou Ki. However, it took only one trip to a mission station ten miles away by bicycle to change his mind. My new catechist had been living in the city and was used to traveling by Jeep.

After the long bicycle trip out to that mission station and a long day of hearing confessions, Mass, interviews, dinner, and other business, it was late evening.

By this time, bicycling was a welcome exercise for me and I just wanted to get home. So, I took off without waiting for anyone else. That was a mistake. None of my other companions waited for my new catechist either. He had to make the ten-mile trip in the dark on the bicycle by himself and he fell along the way.

The next day the new catechist came in and told me about his difficult trip home. He told it in such a humorous way that I didn't realize how upset he was. He left, only to return a few minutes later saying he thought he had hurt his shoulder when he fell; and he requested an x-ray. I told him, "By all means, get an x-ray."

The next day my new catechist told me he had decided he was not physically up to this job and was resigning. He had talked to his wife and, to her great joy, they had decided to move to Seoul.

I was extremely sorry to lose him, but there was nothing I could say to change his mind. I certainly understood his predicament. He had actually made a sacrifice to come to Mou Ki and he certainly could do a lot better financially in Seoul, with much less physical stress.

I sent word out through the diocese, but no one could recommend another catechist. So I turned to Andrew, our assistant catechist. He was a very good carpenter by trade and a very honest man. Andrew not only knew how to build, but he had a great sense of design and had overseen the building of the mission station chapels. I liked him and knew I could trust him completely. He also knew Catholic doctrine very well, so he could contribute to teaching about the Catholic faith.

Andrew was not a "yang ban"—a gentleman. He was a tradesman without a professional education. In South Korea, "gentlemen" were descendants of an educated ruling class. In the Chong Ju province, "gentlemen" had a special status which a tradesman could never achieve. Nevertheless, this carpenter became my catechist during my last year in Mou Ki. Although he was a competent catechist, his heart was really in construction of buildings.

Asking for my tape measure when I was leaving the parish was the only favor Andrew ever requested of me. It was a retractable metal tape measure, one of the tools I had garnered from my dad and had brought with me to South Korea. I was happy to give it to this catechist because I knew he would use it well. I left the rest of my father's box of tools with Father John Murphy, who replaced me when I left for the States at the end of my six-year tour in Korea.

FIRST RETURN VISIT TO THE U.S.

Having completed my first six-year tour in South Korea, I returned to the States in late October 1965 for the required six months stay. Then I was to return to South Korea. This return visit to the States was meant to be a time to rest, to visit family, friends, and classmates, to stay in touch with my home country and the American Church, and to reflect on my life and my mission goals.

In America's larger dioceses, at that time, a priest often served as an assistant pastor in several parishes for between 15 to 30 or more years before becoming a pastor. In South Korea, I had been appointed pastor after serving only two years as an assistant pastor. So, I felt that going to the missions had given me a wonderful, blessed opportunity.

I was quite surprised by what an adjustment it was to return to life in the States. On the flight home, we stopped in Honolulu and stayed in the Maryknoll House there for a day before continuing our journey. I felt overwhelmed by the sheer abundance and variety of food and other products when I went into an ordinary Honolulu supermarket. At that time there was nothing like this in South Korea and it seemed like extreme luxury.

It was the same back in my home town, Akron, Ohio. It took me about six months to get used to the American way of life again: for example, the simple act of discarding things into the trash can. In South Korea, all glass bottles and paper were re-used in some form or other. Nothing was thrown away. We had to make sure we destroyed any labels on the bottles being discarded or they would reappear somewhere advertising a fake product.

In contrast, these items, plus lots of other things, were just discarded in the United States. Only decades later has recycling been promoted in the American consumer society, not so much out of frugality but to reduce the amount of waste going into our landfills and to save our forests and other natural resources.

It took me several months to accept as ordinary the amount and quality of merchandise that was available in the stores. Supermarkets, department stores, malls, and giant book stores were every-where. Bookstores were especially enticing to me. They were an invitation to get lost in vicarious living.

Because my energy level was very low and I wasn't eating well, I visited several doctors who sug-gested taking pep pills. My sister-in-law, Mary Alice, arranged for me to see a special Internist in Akron. This doctor promised he would discover the cause of my symptoms and biopsied my liver, which led to a diagnosis of hepatitis.

Several of my priest colleagues in South Korea had had bouts of hepatitis, so I was not unfamiliar with the disease. We believed that they contracted it from immunizations received in Seoul before return-ing to the States. I had been told that needles were often re-used in South Korean health care facilities.

The usual telltale signs of the disease are extreme fatigue and jaundice, which makes one's skin and the whites of the eyes turn yellow. I asked the doctor why I hadn't turned yellow. He replied that I had a chronic, borderline case that was not severe enough to cause jaundice, but nevertheless was sapping my energy. The remedy was rest for at least a year. So, I was forbidden to return to South Korea at the end of the usual six months. He also prescribed some protein powders.

For the next several months, I helped out at some of the local parishes, saying Mass and hear-ing confessions, but did little else. To my surprise, I found that I could sleep for 24 hours at a time. By summer, I was feeling like my old self and started to petition to return to South Korea. I had enjoyed my work and life there and was eager to return. I had also negotiated permission from Bishop Pardy, the bishop I served under in Korea, to return to language school for more training.

After ten months in the US, with the provision that I would be living in the Maryknoll Center House in Seoul and attending language school for nine months, the doctor gave me permission to return to South Korea. Only after language school was I to be assigned to the physically demanding parish work in the countryside.

MISSION SUPPORT CLUBS

In Summer 1959, just before I was departing for South Korea for the first time, I said Mass at St. Martha's Church on the north side of Akron. After Mass, a couple came back to the sacristy to meet me: Bill Eberhardt, a classmate of mine from St. Mary's High School and his wife, Jean. They were interested in the missions and wanted to know how they could help. Shortly after I arrived in South Korea, Jean formed a Mission Club with several women from St. Martha's Church.

One of the great things they did was to collect medicine samples that I delivered to the Maryknoll sisters' clinic. The medicines were greatly appreciated because the clinic's pharmaceutical supply was usually low and there was always an unending line of people at their door needing care. Jean and the Mission Club members had worked all this out on their own.

In 1966, when I had returned to Akron, I met all the women in the Mission Club. At that time, I was still fairly shy with women, but they were a wonderful group and I was especially grateful for their work. I also spent some long evenings visiting with Jean and Bill Eberhardt at their home. Jean was writing a novel and asked me to critique her writing. I didn't have enough sense to say I really wasn't qualified to do that, but we had some enjoyable times anyway.

When Bill and Jean came to the house to pick me up, my dad always offered them some of his homemade cherry wine. My dad made a small barrel of wine almost every year. When we were kids, my brother Bernard and I used to have to spend days picking the cherries. Dad liked his wine to be sweet, so he always added a lot of sugar to the fermentation process. I thought his wine was too sweet and avoided drinking it. Later I grew to like wine, but preferred good red Merlots and Cabernets. I suspect, though, I might also have come to better appreciate his home-brewed sweet wines.

One really unfortunate incident occurred that involved a woman from Jean Eberhardt's Mission Club. This woman had used material from her wedding dress to make a set of Mass vestments and mailed them to me in South Korea. What I received was a box stuffed with bricks. The vestments had been stolen in transit.

I wrote to Jean to tell her what had happened, but not to the woman directly. I assumed that Jean would share the bad news with her. Sometime after my final return from South Korea, the woman came to me and asked what had happened to her gift of the set of vestments. Only then did I realize that no one had informed her about what had happened. She was crestfallen when I told her. I felt terrible that this was the outcome of her having contributed such a generous gift, and that she had had to wait years to find this out. It was as if her gift wasn't appreciated.

Two other mission support groups were also especially helpful to my work in South Korea. Mrs. Walko started a group in Cleveland. She was a wonderful woman, really dedicated to supporting my mission efforts. I admired her commitment to the missions.

The second group was from the Immaculate Conception parish in the Kenmore section of Akron— my home parish. This group raised the money that enabled me to purchase a vehicle. When I returned to Korea, I ordered a Toyota utility vehicle directly from Japan. Without that vehicle I would never have been able to do the work I did during those years. My biggest regret was that I was never able to personally thank the donors. They made their contributions through my mother and never identified themselves.

My mother, of course, was my biggest supporter during those years. She kept everyone informed of my doings and worked as my stateside secretary. Correspondence was always a chore for me, especially when so much was going on with my work in South Korea. However, I wrote to her and my dad once a week for years. It was only during that last year in South Korea, when I was troubled by the changes in the Church brought about by Vatican Council II, that my letters became more sporadic.

The next three years I spent in South Korea are described in the next chapter. During this time, my thinking about the Church and my place in it changed very gradually. I became increasingly critical of the Church and, together with several other Maryknollers, came to be at odds with our bishop and the Church leadership. The following section describes the Second Vatican Council which affected the Roman Catholic Church and me, in particular, so much at that time.

THE ROMAN CATHOLIC ECUMENICAL COUNCIL, 1962-1965

This Council is more commonly referred to as "Vatican II." The First Vatican Council occurred in 1868, almost 100 years earlier. Ecumenical councils have generally been called to discuss or clarify doctrinal issues. Because these councils involve all levels of the hierarchy, they are considered to be more authoritative than individual papal decrees.

Vatican I declared the Pope to be infallible when making certain formal pronouncements. Some Roman Catholic bishops were so upset by this that they walked out, formed the "Old Catholic Church", and were no longer under papal authority. However, since Vatican I, only two "infallible" pronouncements have been made: those regarding the Immaculate Conception and the Assumption into heaven of the Blessed Virgin Mary.

Pope John XXIII surprised everyone when he called for Vatican Council II in 1961, proclaiming that he wanted an "aggiornamento", an updating or taking stock of the Church in the context of the modern world. He talked about opening the windows and letting fresh air into the Roman Catholic Church.

Pope John XXIII was aware of the conservative prophets of doom among the Vatican curia (the Roman Catholic Church's central bureaucracy) who opposed any sweeping changes in the Church. His purpose was to have the council fathers focus more on pastoral issues affecting Catholics and their lives in the world than on doctrinal issues.

Vatican Council II took place from 1962 to 1965, during my first tour in Korea. Over 2,000 bishops and cardinals attended the sessions, including all of the South Korean bishops. They were the voting members. Experts (usually theologians) who informed and advised the bishops attended, as well as religious sisters and members of the laity.

The Council produced sixteen powerful documents which pointed toward radical change in how the Church perceived itself, worshipped, and related to the modern world. Perhaps the most visible and well-known changes were in the liturgy. The centuries old Latin Mass was set aside and was replaced by liturgies in the vernacular, the native language of each geographic region. This upset some Catholics who, even today, crave the Latin Mass. So, it is still offered in certain churches.

The priest formerly celebrated Mass with his back to the congregation. Now, the altar and the priest were to face the people. The people were no longer passively attending Mass, but were expected to actively participate in the Scripture readings, the singing, and the reciting of prayers and responses. This was intended to help the faithful realize that the Mass was a celebration of their unity, their oneness as the Mystical Body of Christ in today's world.

Another major change was the recognition of the laity, by virtue of their baptism, as equal members of the Church—just as holy as the clergy. The Church was clearly identified as comprising all of the faithful, the people of God, and not just the hierarchy. Collegiality and dialogue became the rules of the day and were meant to extend from the Pope down to every church member, including lay persons. The Pope was supposed to listen to the bishops, the bishops to the priests, the priests to the faithful, and the faithful to each other.

Freedom of religion was proclaimed, as well as new respect for other churches and faith traditions—including the Jewish and Eastern religions. Triumphal attitudes, which insisted that "there was no salvation outside the Catholic Church" because it was the only true religion, were no longer believed or taught. John Courtney Murray, an American Jesuit, had a lot to do with formulating the document on freedom of religion. He basically wrote it.

The Index, the old list of censored books, disappeared. Certain theologians who had been silenced were suddenly being acknowledged and supported, including: Yves Congar, a French Dominican priest and theologian who had a major influence on the Council teachings on ecumenism; John Courtney Murray, as mentioned above; and Teilhard de Chardin, a French Jesuit who was a philosopher, paleontologist, geologist, and avid believer in evolution.

Pope John XXIII recommended that the ministries of congregations of religious women become more involved in the world. Many nuns discarded their religious garb, moved out of their convents and into apartments, and took jobs in a variety of social services. Some did this while remaining religious sisters, while others left their congregations. The laity were now encouraged to read and study the Scriptures, and began to study theology as well.

Just a few of the changes that affected me have been mentioned. The changes brought about by Vatican II were welcomed by many with great excitement and enthusiasm. While conservative Catholics were upset, thinking there were too many drastic changes, more liberal Catholics felt that there should have been even more changes. They felt that some of the documents were the result of too many compromises. This polarization in the Roman Catholic Church has continued over the last sixty years.

Pope John XXIII died before the Council ended and his successor, Pope Paul VI, supported the outcomes of Vatican Council II in general. In regard to the issue of artificial contraception, however, a commission of "experts" (including both theologians and lay persons) was tasked with considering this issue in light of current scientific knowledge so as to come up with a recommendation regarding the Church's ban on artificial contraception.

After their deliberations, the commission favored removing the ban on artificial contraception; however, Pope Paul VI listened to other advisers who claimed he would lose all credibility if he changed the Church's teaching on this matter. In 1968, he wrote *Humanae Vitae,* an encyclical or letter to all the bishops of the Roman Catholic Church, which mandated continuing the ban on artificial contraception.

The result among the faithful was unexpected and totally surprising. A majority of Catholics have not accepted the Pope's teaching. They have followed their own consciences regarding the use of birth control to this day. While there are those who obey the Pope in this matter, many others do not.

This brief review of the impact of Vatican Council II on the Roman Catholic Church has been presented to help the reader understand the profound effect it had on me when I returned to South Korea in September 1966.

CHAPTER 4

Return to Korea

WHEN I RETURNED TO SOUTH KOREA IN Fall 1966, I found that the language school was different from the one I had attended years before in Maryknoll's Center House. The Franciscans had built and staffed a school in downtown Seoul and all the mission groups sent new arrivals there for language school.

Besides Americans, students from New Zealand, Ireland, Germany, France and Switzerland were also in attendance. We were exposed to various Korean teachers who drilled us on different aspects of the language. Overall, it was a wonderful experience and it helped me improve my language skills.

I was surprised I had missed so many of the ordinary modes of expression. Yet, despite the added training, I still did not understand the ordinary, everyday language of the people as much as I would have liked. The language barrier continued to be a source of frustration for me.

PO UN

When my studies at the language school ended in June 1967, I returned to the Chong Ju diocese and Bishop Pardy suggested some possible assignments for me. One was to a parish that a Maryknoll priest, Father Phil, was leaving for his stateside assignment. This meant he would not return to that parish. Father Phil advised me against taking the assignment. I knew that he had endured some sort of major trouble shortly before leaving, so I took his advice. I was never told what the major trouble was. Since I was not going there, I did not see any need to find out.

Bishop Pardy assigned a newly-ordained Korean priest to that parish. This young man was a very smart and capable person. So, despite his lack of parish experience, I was confident that he would handle the situation well. I believe he did as I never heard about the problem after that.

Father Jerry Farrell was also leaving for his stateside assignment. But his case was an exception to Bishop Pardy's rule about Maryknollers not returning to the same parish after returning from their stateside visits. Father Jerry had just built a modern church for his Po Un parish, which also included a small hospital/clinic for which he was responsible.

The hospital/clinic was staffed by sisters from a community whose motherhouse was in Germany, as well as by some Korean sisters. Father Jerry was a medical doctor before becoming a priest, so he understood the needs of the hospital/clinic. Because of these special circumstances, Father Jerry would be returning as pastor at Po Un on return from his stateside visit.

Although stateside assignments were usually for six months, Father Jerry had also signed up for some type of study, possibly focused on pastoral counseling in a hospital setting. So, I was assigned to fill in for one year until he returned.

The Po Un rectory and church were built on a hill above the town which was surrounded by mountains. The church could be seen from just about anywhere in the valley. It had been designed by a German Benedictine and built according to the new Vatican II liturgical reforms. The altar was situated in the middle of the semi-round church, allowing all the people to sit close to the altar. It was a beautiful church and the view from the hilltop was spectacular.

One of my first duties at Po Un was to supervise modifications to the rectory. This involved obtaining a small steel beam, something that was not readily available in South Korea in the 1960s. Someone eventually directed me to a city outside our province where I was able to obtain the beam. The rest of the work involved building around it. Since I was not paying for the project, I only needed to spend time supervising it.

I also inherited a major problem of dissension in the parish. For years there had been two main catechists. Since one main catechist ran the show in most parishes, having two main catechists was an invitation to competition, jealousy, and eventual disaster.

Sometime in the year before I arrived, one catechist had accused the other of taking kickbacks during the building of the new church. Feeling unjustly accused, the second catechist had resigned and refused to attend church anymore. The people in the parish were also divided. Some were very loyal to the first catechist and others remained loyal to the second catechist, even though he no longer attended church.

I arrived at Po Un totally unaware of this situation. At a meeting soon after my arrival attended by several church leaders—including some of the catechists from the outlying mission stations—the remaining main catechist began an angry diatribe. I didn't understand everything he was saying, but knew it had nothing to do with the purpose of the meeting and there didn't seem to be any end to his venting. So, I interrupted and asked him to stop. He did and the meeting then went on as planned.

Later, I learned that his angry diatribe concerned the perceived sins of the second main catechist. Because I hadn't been there for the original accusations, and since the other catechist was no longer attending church, I didn't understand the remaining catechist's need to carry on against him. Little did I know how much I had offended my remaining main catechist. My interruption and sitting him down was a great loss of face as far as he was concerned.

I didn't apologize, not realizing that there was any need to do so. I did discuss with him that his job was to attend to the catechetical work of the parish and not to carry on this vendetta against the other catechist. He promised he would not do it again.

Everything was quiet for a couple of weeks, until one Sunday after Mass someone came running into the office, upset about some fighting going on outside. I ran outside and found the main catechist in the middle of an angry verbal interchange with some of the parishioners about his animosity toward the other catechist. I was enraged. I reminded him that he was violating his promise and led him into the office, followed by his wife. His wife grabbed hold of the door knob and refused to let go, which provoked me to slap her wrist. This, of course, was a very big no-no. I then let the main catechist know how angry I was about his behavior.

The situation had now gone from bad to worse. I knew I was in trouble, and too personally-involved to repair the damage. I called Bishop Pardy and asked him to intervene. He sent a Korean layman who worked for him supervising construction work in the diocese. I took this as an indication that the bishop wasn't taking this too seriously.

Sending a Korean layman, instead of an American priest, to handle the situation turned out to be a good move. He arrived and interviewed everyone. I didn't know what he reported to the bishop or what he said to the catechist, but he told me that I had to apologize for slapping the hand of the catechist's wife. I found this hard to do, but I did apologize.

Shortly after this, the main catechist informed me he was resigning and moving out of the diocese. I accepted his resignation, but it was still not over.

To show their solidarity with the main catechist, a catechist from the largest mission station also resigned, as did my cook. Although I didn't know the mission catechist very well, I had nothing against him. I accepted his resignation as a way to reduce the payroll since I was having trouble meeting all the expenses of such a large parish.

Losing the cook was another matter. I sent out word to the other parishes and Father Dan said he knew a woman who had had some culinary training with the Maryknoll sisters. She was a nice person and needed the job, so I hired her. She turned out to be a terrible cook, but we stuck with her. For example, one time when a group of Maryknollers gathered in the rectory at Po Un to celebrate one of their birthdays, this cook prepared a beautifully decorated cake for the occasion. However, when the men took their first bite of the cake, they almost choked on it. Then we found out that the beautiful frosting was made of lard!!

I never did find out what had gone on between the two main catechists. I was never shown any proof of wrongdoing. So, I felt that I was in no position to pass judgment on either one. As far as I was concerned, it was over and it was time to focus the parish on doing the works of mercy that good Christians should do. It was a consolation to me to overhear a parishioner remark that I didn't stand by quietly, but intervened and got things resolved. She wasn't talking to me and I didn't think she even knew that I heard her.

I didn't hire another main catechist. The assistant catechist, a very bright young man and a dedicated worker, assumed his duties. We had many long talks about how to help the parish and, especially, how to develop an awareness of the social needs of the people. As a result, we got some of the parishioners engaged in attending to the needs of the sick, working on water projects, and other good works.

Some months later, at the urging of the young catechist, I visited the former second main catechist who was still living in town but not attending church. He was very cordial and friendly. I invited and even urged him to return to the parish, but he had been hurt badly by the accusations against him and didn't feel he could do so.

During my stay in Po Un, Father Art Grubert was assigned as assistant pastor. Father Art had arrived in South Korea six years after I had. He was a most interesting person who loved to sing and enjoyed attending any event or party where there was music and the opportunity to sing. Since I couldn't carry a tune, I greatly admired his singing ability.

Besides Father Art's presence making life more fun, he was a hard-working, dedicated priest. During the few months we were together in Po Un, Father Art reached out ecumenically by inviting ministers from the other church denominations in town, Protestant and non-Christian as well, to meet once a month.

Mock funeral procession after blessing of new parish hearse, 1968

A year later, when I was in Yong Dong and he was still in Po Un, Father Art would stop by for a visit. By then I had gotten a record player and purchased some Peter, Paul and Mary records. When Fathers Art and/ or John Hallinan stopped by, the first thing either of them did was to play one of those records. Father Art's favorite was *I Dig Rock and Roll Music*. He loved to sing along and his entire countenance lit up when he did so. Art, John and I played those records over and over again. They spoke to me like no other music ever had.

Me and parish kids in utility vehicle donated by Akron, Ohio parishioners

Church workers gathered for a picnic, Po Un 1967

YONG DONG AND THE PIG PROJECTS

When Father Jerry Farrell returned from the States, my time at Po Un was up. In 1968 I was reassigned to the neighboring parish of Yong Dong as pastor. Yong Dong was near the southern tip of the diocese, but it was on both the main highway and the railroad line between Seoul and Pusan. There were five parishes in what we called the "southern tier" of the diocese. Father John Hallinan was stationed ten miles south of Yong Dong. Father Vince Hoffman was ten miles north. Po Un, where Father Jerry Farrell had just returned, was ten miles east. Father Fred Krampart was pastor of a parish on another road back in the country that didn't lead to any major destination.

Post-Baptism on Holy Saturday, Yong Dong, 1969

Me recovering after a mountain hike with friends, 1968

The total area included three counties in the Chong Ju province. It was a large and highly populated area. Yong Dong was the most centrally-located of the five parishes, so the other priests passed through Yong Dong a lot. My rectory at Yong Dong was a natural gathering place.

Father Vince Hoffman was the oldest and most experienced priest among us. Father Vince called us all together and strongly pushed for some coopera-tive activity. There were some ongoing social works in the parishes such as a clinic, a farm, and an old folks' home. And Father Vince was in the process of building a three-story hospital. But he wanted us to attempt something as a group that would benefit all five parishes.

We started by having a catechist working with Father Gerald Kennedy conduct a survey. The pur-pose of the survey was to ask the farmers, who made up the bulk of the population, what they felt was needed to help raise their standard of living.

Conducting the survey was not easy because the parishes were so spread out and travel and commu-nications were especially difficult. I arranged for Father Kennedy's trained catechist to come to Yong Dong and I called in all the volunteer catechists from the parish mission stations to meet him and help get the survey started.

Some of these volunteers might have come by bus, but most walked miles to get to Yong Dong. Travel was always a big deal. At that time the only paved road was the two-lane major highway between Seoul and Pusan. Otherwise, there were only dirt roads and the people traveled by bus, by bicycle, by truck, and mostly by foot.

I emphasized to the catechists how this survey would, hopefully, lead to some important project to help the volunteers in the future. They were anxious to hear about it and waited and waited for the trained catechist to arrive. I was on the telephone trying to find out where he was and why he wasn't in Yong Dong. (Telephones were very recent additions to the countryside.) By the end of the morning he still hadn't arrived, so I had to send everyone home. This important meeting had just become a waste of everyone's time.

The trained catechist finally showed up the next day. I don't remember his reason for not being there the day we had arranged, but I remember how angry I was. It was not only an embarrassment, but terribly disappointing. He no sooner arrived than I lit into him about how many men had come long distances from the out-stations and waited all morning for nothing. We argued and he walked out.

I'm not sure now whether I told him to leave or whether he was angry enough to decide to leave on his own. At that point I didn't care. Five minutes later there was a knock on the door. He had returned and asked if we could start over. We did so and, thereafter, we had a good working relationship. But I always regretted that those men had waited so long for nothing.

The results of the parish surveys made clear the need for help to raise the parishioners' standard of living, but no specific ideas were brought forth as to how to accomplish that. The next step in our group effort was to decide what kind of project would benefit the farmers. We decided to travel around South Korea to see what had been done by others.

It quickly became apparent that the most promising project would be to introduce the Landrace pig. Father Mike Bransfield, my classmate, had done so in his parish in the Inchon diocese. Father John Hallinan and I then flew to Je Ju Do, an island off the southern tip of South Korea where a Columban Order priest had started a very large pig farm.

I had never flown anywhere in South Korea before. My initial anxiety quickly melted away. The plane wasn't a little puddle jumper, but a decent-sized plane flown by Korean Air.

We spent two days in Je Ju Do. The first night we spent several hours in the rectory talking with the Irish priest about the pig farm and all the difficulties and successes he had experienced in getting it off the ground and keeping it going.

One of the major things he warned us about was not to police the project in any way. If Americans (or any foreigners) set themselves up to police a project, it then became the Koreans' game to outfox the foreigner. Anyone who could steal from or outfox the foreigner would gain great credit or "face" before his peers.

The next morning we rose early, said Mass, and had breakfast. Then we waited for a couple of hours in the same room we'd been in the night before, only now it wasn't heated. I didn't tolerate the cold very well. Father John and I shivered, talked and read a little. Mostly, we just waited.

Our good Irish friend had slept-in late and didn't meet with us until almost noon. However, he then gave us a good tour of his pig farm and continued to tell us about his experiences and what was necessary to make a pig farm work.

One interesting thing he did to solve his water problem was to lay piping down to collect snow melt from the mountain that dominated the center of the island. We eventually had our own water problem trying to dig a well but, unfortunately, had no access to any mountain snow. We flew out later that afternoon armed with some very valuable and practical information.

Landrace pigs raised outside my Church in Yong Dong, 1969

To make a long story short, we decided to make the pig project a Co-op and combine it with establishment of a Credit Union—an idea supported by all five parishes. Only members of the Credit Union could share in the pig project. The parishes urged their members to join, even if they only had a few pennies to deposit. The Credit Union became the educational instrument for the whole project. It was decided to center the pig farm and Credit Union in Yong Dong because it was the most central of the five parishes and was on the main road to Seoul, our future market.

Our biggest obstacle, of course, was financial. Where were we going to get the money to start the project? We required the members to contribute to the Credit Union, but they couldn't possibly come up with the amount of funding it would take to get a pig farm started.

We got donations from Maryknoll and from Oxfam, a global organization that fights inequality, poverty, and injustice. Father Jerry Farrell had a classmate who had left Maryknoll to join a French missionary order and then had been transferred to the Pusan diocese under Bishop Choi. I accompanied Father Jerry to Pusan to meet with his classmate who had organized a very successful stateside fundraising campaign by letter for Bishop Choi. Father Jerry did the talking and explained in detail what we were attempting to do. I just observed. We subsequently received a helpful donation from Bishop Choi thanks to Father Jerry's classmate.

We were then able to buy some land next to the parish property on which to build the pig styes, buy the first few pigs, and start the farm. Earlier we had convened some men from each parish to discuss the project and help us to actually implement it. They elected a young man named Simon from Father John Hallinan's parish to be their leader and spokesperson. He had some training and experience in running a credit union.

We hired Simon to run the Credit Union and manage the pig project. Simon understood the concept of a credit union and he knew how to make it work on a personal level. He was also a natural manager and competently managed the details involved in operating a pig farm.

The people had been contributing to neighborhood connections to assist with providing funds for weddings and funerals. We constantly heard stories of how this money was lost, stolen, misused, or simply ran out. So, I was amazed at how well Simon was able to handle the Credit Union collecting and lending processes among these very poor people.

We also hired an agricultural expert who had graduated at the top of his class from the main agricultural university in Seoul. He had helped Father Mike Bransfield get his pig farm started. I was sorry that I couldn't remember his name because he played a very important part in the project's start-up. He really knew how to raise Landrace pigs.

Traditionally, Koreans had raised a type of pig that survived in extremely filthy conditions and lived on whatever scraps the farmer could afford.

Somehow, these pigs had developed an immunity that enabled them to survive under these adverse conditions. But the local families could usually raise only one pig at a time and it took a year or more for these pigs to grow to maturity.

The Landrace pig was developed in Denmark in the 1880s and Denmark protected the purity of the breed for decades. The United States eventually was granted a limited number to cross-breed, but was not allowed to breed any pure stock. Denmark didn't release its restrictions until 1949. Then American farmers were able to import and breed pure Landrace pigs.

Landrace pigs are known for producing more rib, loin, and ham cuts of meat. I never knew how the Landrace pigs first got to South Korea and they were not well known in the country. We were among the first to introduce the Landrace pig to the Chong Ju province.

The requirements for raising Landrace pigs are quite different from the way Koreans traditionally raised pigs. Landrace pigs need a clean environment and proper food. People were educated about this through the Credit Union. This training was especially important for the women, because they were the ones who usually fed and cared for the pigs on a daily basis.

As previously mentioned, the pig project was organized as a Co-op and a group from each parish decided to join. Our agricultural expert traveled by bus to each parish, supervised the building of the right kind of pig styes and instructed the farmers on the absolute necessity of keeping them clean. Then each group was given several baby Landrace pigs to raise.

The Co-op provided the proper food and the farmers were told that, if they fed the pigs proper food in the correctly measured amount, the pigs would not only survive but would grow to market size in six months. The Co-op would then transport the pigs to market in Seoul, where the farmers could get a better price for them.

The system worked. Only one group failed because, instead of feeding the pigs with the proper food, they sold the feed and fed the pigs their traditional scraps. Of course, those pigs did not thrive and were not taken to market. Those farmers were then disqualified from being future Landrace pig farmers.

Another example of our agricultural expert's effort to ensure survival of the Landrace pigs was his decision to bypass the distribution system for the government's free cholera vaccine program. The cholera vaccine had to be kept cold to maintain its effectiveness. The problem was that, in its passage from Seoul to rural communities and then out to the farms, the vaccine often ended up becoming too warm and, thus, became ineffective. Our agricultural expert went to Seoul and obtained the vaccine himself. He was then careful to keep the vaccine refrigerated until, when he returned, he went to each parish and inoculated every Landrace pig with the vaccine himself.

Getting the proper food for the pigs was another important task. We found out that we could get high quality protein food for the pigs by buying fish directly from the fishermen in Pusan. We had to get a truck (one of the contributions we begged for) to transport the fish shipments from Pusan to Yong Dong, and later to transport the pigs to market in Seoul.

We received our first shipment of fish before we had a barn or any place to store it, so Father John Hallinan volunteered his parish hall. The fish had to be spread out all over the floor to allow them to dry out. This worked very well. The only downside was the everlasting stink in the parish hall that Father John's parishioners had to endure.

All the priests in the Southern Tier contributed to the pig project. They supported the Credit Union and Co-op in their own parishes. All major decisions, such as collecting the finances and hiring our experts, were made together. It really was a team effort, but I think Father John Hallinan was probably the most excited by the project and stayed the most involved.

We had one failure that cost us some goodwill. Father Fred Krampart had started raising a few Landrace pigs before we got our pig project in gear. He felt it only right that we include his pigs in our pig project.

Our agricultural expert didn't want to do that. He had very carefully selected all the pigs for the project, including the breeding sows that produced the piglets that were sent to the farmers to raise. He was especially careful to select pigs that would meet the expected growth gains in six months. Although they were Landrace piglets, our agricultural expert was reluctant to take on Father Fred's pigs because he knew they were inferior to the Coop's Landrace pigs.

The decision was made to include Father Fred's pigs only if they met the six-month required weight gains that the rest of the farmers had to meet. Unfortunately, his pigs did not meet the weight gain requirement and, thus, were rejected. There were some negative reactions from other Maryknoll colleagues who asked how we could do that to a fellow Maryknoller. However, the pig project was in the Co-op's control, not the priests', and everybody was being held to the same standards.

An important key to the success of the pig project was that everything was put into the name of the Credit Union and Co-op. We supplied the initial money, as well as the impetus to get it going, and continued to be supporters and consultants. But the project was turned over to the Co-op completely.

This was a major change from the way social works were conducted by the diocese. Traditionally, every building and institution was put in the name of the bishop and owned by him. And all the diocesan finances were controlled by the bishop. Thus, financial support could be stopped, siphoned off, increased or decreased according to the decisions of the bishop and the needs of the diocese. Because our pig project was put entirely in the name of the Credit Union and Co-op, neither the bishop nor the priests could interfere with how the finances and resources were used.

Since the pig project was set up in Yong Dong, I was available most of the time and was usually the first priest Simon would consult, especially concerning financial decisions. I relayed all major concerns to the rest of the priests, who remained very interested in the progress of the pig project. They would often visit to check on its progress.

Having had no farming or co-op or credit union experience and no natural organizing ability, taking on the whole project would have been overwhelming for me to even think about. It only became a reality because Father Vince Hoffman urged us to work together to do something beyond our individual capability and efforts, and because of the fantastic support and cooperation of the other priests in the Southern Tier. Nor would it have been successful without the equally hard work and dedication of Simon and our agricultural expert.

Large projects are usually begun with high hopes and much fanfare. Sometimes they succeed and sometimes they don't. And there is always some legitimate skepticism voiced, especially in the beginning. But from the very start I was especially confident that this project would succeed. My confidence was based on the personalities, know-how, expertise, and dedication of Simon and our agricultural expert. None of us priests were farmers and none of us had experience raising pigs, but Simon and our agricultural expert knew what they were doing and were determined to make it work.

I don't know the ultimate fate of the pig project or whether it is still in existence today, over 60 years later. But it was still operating successfully 20 years later and had had a very positive impact on the local economy. And the Co-op received some government recognition for doing so. Simon was still managing it, but our agricultural expert had left. He had told me that his dream was to eventually raise cattle, not pigs. So, it did not surprise me to hear that he had emigrated to Canada.

WINDS OF CHANGE:
RE-THINKING MY VOCATION

The progress of the Credit Union and Co-op was important, but it was really an aside. I still had my normal duties as pastor. And I was personally experiencing a lot of inner struggle related to the changes the whole Church was experiencing as a result of the Second Vatican Council that ended in 1965. There was a lot of intellectual ferment throughout the Church and, most particularly for me, among the Maryknollers in South Korea.

When I returned to South Korea in Fall 1966, men were leaving the priesthood—not just in Korea—but throughout the American Church. At that time, I had no intention of ever leaving the priesthood. I enjoyed the work in South Korea. I was moved by and inspired by the Korean people. As far as I could see, my future was in South Korea.

However, the intellectual turmoil and changes taking place in the Church were affecting me, as well as many other Maryknoll missioners in South Korea. At the time there were two major concerns. The first was about how we, as missionaries, should begin to live out the changes promulgated by Vatican Council II. The second had to do with the continuing requirement of mandatory celibacy for Roman Catholic priests.

The Vatican Council II documents indicated that we Roman Catholics needed to adjust our attitudes towards other faiths and cultures, including Protestant, Jewish, non-Christian, Muslim, and Eastern churches. And we, as Roman Catholic missionaries working in foreign lands and cultures, had to question our goals and the validity of any triumphal proselytizing. Triumphal proselytizing meant trying to convert people by attesting that the Roman Catholic Church was better and truer than any other religion. Pope John XXIII was telling us to get involved with the modern world and to pay attention to the needs of the people.

The Maryknollers working In the Chong Ju diocese questioned what the bishop was doing. Perhaps the best critique I heard was Father Gerry Kennedy's suggestion that our Maryknoll bishop was trying to develop a diocese patterned on an American diocese, such as the Brooklyn diocese. Didn't South Korea, being a different country with a very different non-Christian culture, deserve a different approach?

The conflicting views came to a head when the bishop called a meeting to elect priests to positions on certain diocesan committees. A number of priests believed that there should be some dialogue about whether these particular committees were the best for serving the needs of our South Korean diocese. I don't remember what the particular committees were, but they probably included youth and catechetical committees along with a few more. There was nothing wrong with them, but this group of priests questioned whether there could be some committees formed that would be more meaning-ful to the average Korean parishioner. For example, what about a liturgy committee or a Korean culture committee to enlist more Korean input? We simply asked for some discussion of these ideas.

Bishop Pardy was not present at the meeting, but he had instructed his vicar general to hold the specified committee elections, stipulating that there would be no discussion; the men would only vote. Hearing that, some of us spontaneously got up and walked out. That brought an end to the meeting without any voting.

There were probably just as many priests at the meeting who sided with the bishop as there were those who walked out. Those who stayed considered those of us who walked out to be wrong and disobedient, since the bishop had left orders and it was our duty to fol-low them. One of them told me that he thought the walk-out was planned and not spontaneous. However, no one had told me of any plan to walk out. It just felt like the right thing to do at the time.

In any case, the bishop called a meeting of those who had walked out. There was a good discussion and we got a lot off our minds, but the bishop didn't give in one iota and we left in a stalemate. Another meeting for elections to the committees was held with the bishop present and the elections proceeded with no discussion and no interruptions or walk-outs. In effect, the men did what the bishop asked.

The upshot of all this was that news of the walkout spread and we were now labeled as reb-els. You just did not disobey your bishop or rebel against him. The bishop handled the split among the priests by sending the discontents as far from him as he could—that is, to the Southern and Northern Tiers of the Chong Ju diocese. I don't remember any expressed decision on his part but, in actuality, all communication stopped. Bishop Pardy basically ignored us priests in the Southern Tier. He sent us no orders and we didn't tell him what we were doing.

I didn't feel like I was a rebel. I felt unhappy about the whole situation, not just the division between the priests in the diocese. The documents of Vatican Council II had turned everything upside down. The ideas and attitudes about the Church and religion that had governed my behavior up until then were all in question. In the Catholic elementary and high schools I had attended, and during my nine years of training for the priesthood, I had studied hard and learned the "truth" and based my life on that truth. Now I had to question what I believed. This left me very angry. I felt like I had lost all my certitude.

Because of all the Vatican II changes, and the rift that developed between the Maryknollers in South Korea who supported the changes and those who resisted them, a Maryknoll council member from the States was sent to dialogue with us and listen to what the men were thinking.

We had a general meeting in Seoul of all the Maryknoll men in South Korea. The priests working in the Chong Ju diocese were very concerned about how the relationships between many of the men and Bishop Pardy had deteriorated. There were most likely other Maryknollers who thought that the problem was simply the refusal of these men to obey the bishop.

The Maryknollers in Inchon were more concerned with the celibacy rule and the fact that so many men were leaving the priesthood, or staying but getting involved with women. In any case, the men were polarized and many were leaving the priesthood. The priests who were leaving were agreeing with Vatican II that marriage and the lay life were as good and holy a way to live as was the priesthood. They were quite willing to remain as priests in active ministry, but only if they could be married men who treasured the human love of another. The Pope and the Vatican, however, said "No, the rule of celibacy must be retained."

I knew and had heard stories about priests having mistresses or resorting to alcohol or dying bitter and unhappy. The men who were leaving chose love, rather than facing a future of loneliness and hypocrisy. By their actions they were also saying that women deserved love within a sacred marriage. That was putting the choice of a woman in marriage on an equal footing with the choice of the priesthood. There are many hierarchs who still don't accept the premise that, as human beings, women are equal to men and should be treated as such by the Church.

At the meeting of all Maryknollers serving in South Korea, I also remembered Bishop Pardy's vicar general standing up to talk about Maryknoll's new constitution. It had been revised to be in line with the Second Vatican Council documents. He wasn't talking for the bishop or as the vicar general, but simply as a fellow Maryknoll priest, when he expressed concern about the new Maryknoll constitution. He stated that he trembled as he read it. He felt that it was heretical and that the Vatican would never approve it.

I didn't remember what, in particular, the vicar general thought was heretical in the new Maryknoll constitution and it would have been unfair of me to guess at it many years later. However, the Vatican did approve Maryknoll's new constitution. This was another example of the intensity of the rift among the priests due to the difficulty some men had in accepting the changes, and confusion regarding what was truly heretical or not.

Another task we took on in the Southern Tier, without seeking the permission of the bishop, was to begin contributing to the education of the sisters working in our parishes. Many of them had never completed middle or high school. In most cases this was due to the poverty of their families and their religious communities. In the past it didn't matter, since most of the people they were working with also had very little education, especially the women. But, as South Korea became modernized, more young women were continuing their education through middle and high school.

Our sisters needed to be able to match the basic education of other young women so as to function effectively in their teaching and social service roles. As a result, Father Vince Hoffman contacted a Catholic school in Seoul and arranged for us to send some of the sisters there for further study.

Bishop Pardy probably would have refused permission to educate the nuns. I never spoke to him about this issue, but I knew that some people believed it was better if the sisters didn't get too much education. I was told that the bishop didn't believe in contributing to their education since, "if they get educated, they will leave the sisterhood." I considered it terribly unfair not to properly train the sisters for the work they were doing.

Although he didn't communicate directly with us priests in the Southern Tier, Bishop Pardy questioned his other priests and tried to stay aware of what we were doing. But he continued to ignore us and did not interfere with our activities.

One of the downsides of this situation was that the bishop controlled the diocesan finances and no diocesan monies came our way except those due to us by law. This affected Father Vince Hoffman the most because he ran out of money while building a hospital. The structure was three stories high, but the project was stalled and the bishop was not about to help.

I felt that Fathers Kennedy and Hoffman were the most visionary of the priests in the diocese. They questioned the bishop's policies more than others, but I don't recall them ever fomenting any rebellion or trying to organize any of us to oppose the bishop. However, they certainly believed that they had a right to question and disagree with those in authority.

I experienced another incident during that time that puzzled me for years. Three or four priests from the Southern Tier had gathered in the rectory at Yong Dong. They may have been there because of the pig Co-op or they may have just been making a social call. There was a knock on the door and the bishop's vicar general came in. He declined a drink, saying that he had been sent by the bishop on official business.

The vicar general told me that the bishop heard that I was teaching heresy and it had to stop. Was I surprised! I was totally unaware of having taught any heresy and didn't know what he was talking about. A couple of the other priests joined in to challenge the vicar general.

After a short, but heated, discussion, the vicar general told me I had to promise that I would not teach any heresy in the future. If I couldn't promise this, he warned that the bishop would suspend me from my position as pastor at the Yong Dong parish. He insisted that the bishop considered this to be a very serious matter. I responded that I was not aware of having taught heresy and certainly promised that I would not do so in future.

When trying to figure out what heresy I might have been teaching, I could only think of the very ordinary Sunday homilies that I preached each week. They didn't come close to including any heretical ideas. The vicar general accepted my promise and left immediately. I thought he seemed very uncomfortable throughout the encounter and was relieved that I made the promise.

Note that I was accused of heresy, but was never informed as to what the particular heresy was or who was making the accusation. Nor was I given a chance to defend myself. I simply had to promise not to do it again or I was out.

Over the next 40 years, I continued to wonder about what heresy I was thought to have committed. Then, while pondering over and writing about my time in South Korea for this book, it finally occurred to me what the probable cause of the whole incident was.

When I was stationed at Po Un, a woman came to see me and told me she was pregnant. Her husband had died years before. She had two or three children and they were extremely poor. To my knowledge, she had no consistent income, which was not unusual for a woman with no husband.

I had advised other women in the same predicament and had always firmly insisted that they could not have an abortion. I remembered that one of these woman came to see me after her child's birth to very proudly show me her new son. She may not have been as proud if her child had been a girl but, in this case, she was very happy.

This woman from Po Un, however, was extremely upset. She didn't know how she could have the baby. I listened and really felt empathy for her predicament. Being so poor she didn't know how she could have and raise another child. I couldn't tell her what to do. I didn't tell her she had to have the baby. I didn't tell her to have the abortion. I just listened. I left the decision to her.

She left the rectory and I left Po Un shortly thereafter. So, I never heard of the outcome. At the time I was not aware of any adoption process or the possibility of finding ways to subsidize her financial status. Only later in life did I become aware of other options that I could have suggested to her.

Some weeks later, I mentioned this incident to another Maryknoll priest as an example of how my thinking was changing. Previously, I had always been adamant that there never was an excuse to have an abortion. In this case, I was not able to say that. Only many years later did I realize that the Maryknoll priest I had talked with about this situation must have told the bishop what I had done, and that this situation constituted my "heresy."

When I left Yong Dong and South Korea toward the end of October 1969, I expected to return to South Korea. But I also had some doubt about this in the back of my mind. Shortly after I left, the first batch of pigs had reached their sixth month weight and were about to be shipped off to market. Father John Hallinan organized a pig roast so the people could taste how good their meat was. By then I was back in the States, so I missed the celebration.

When I left South Korea in 1969 I was angry with the Church, especially because of the opposition to change and the polarization among the Maryknollers. I had talked about the possibility of leaving, but I really was too scared to do it. I was not in a relation- ship with or in love with any woman, so that was not a motivating factor. I was in a state of questioning and wondering about everything I believed. Nothing seemed clear to me.

In late December, I started attending a Pastoral Counseling Program taught by an Episcopal priest at St. Luke's Hospital in Upper Manhattan in New York

City. In addition to attending classes, we were also assigned chaplain duties in the hospital in order to put into practice what we were being taught.

In the Maryknoll seminary we were taught that hospital work mainly involved distributing communion, administering the last rites, and hearing confessions. The focus of pastoral counseling, however, was on the need to relate to the people as they were and respond to their needs. . .not just to dispense the sacraments.

Taking the pastoral counseling course was exhilarating for me because it was concerned with the psychology of relating to people. In college I had taken an introductory psychology course which quickly surveyed the many branches of psychology but did not go into any depth.

The psychology I was learning at St. Luke's was completely new to me. It was a whole branch of knowledge to which I'd never been exposed. I wondered why Maryknoll had never taught me any of this discipline because it would have been so useful in counseling my parishioners. I felt that I could use all the psychology I could learn, so I opted for a second semester of the program, thus extending my three-month stateside visit by another three months.

During one of our February classes I was sounding off about how upset I was with the Church and, if things didn't get better, I would be leaving the priesthood. One of my classmates, a New York City seminarian, looked at me and simply said, "You've already left." The class ended and everyone left. I sat there, stunned, reflecting that the seminarian was right. I had already left. I just needed to accept the fact and stop denying it.

The next day I wrote to my parents that I had decided to leave Maryknoll and the priesthood. It was the hardest letter I ever wrote because I knew it would hurt them and grievously disappoint them. Then I wrote to Maryknoll to ask for a one-year leave of absence. I was trying to give myself time before finalizing my decision, in case I should discover that it wasn't really what I wanted.

My third letter was to my superior in Korea, telling him that I was taking a leave of absence. Finally, I wrote to the priests in the Southern Tier to tell them I would not be returning. I felt pretty sure that it was only a matter of time before some of them would also leave Maryknoll and this turned out to be the case. After two or three years, Father Jerry Farrell was the only Southern Tier priest who remained in South Korea.

John Hallinan left Maryknoll about one year later and Art Grubert left two years later. After Art left, and without help from John, he met and married John's sister, Maureen. Eventually they ended up at the University of Notre Dame where Art counseled foreign students and Maureen taught, did research, and occupied a prestigious chair. Tragically, Art developed a neurodegenerative disease and died in 2010.

John and Art had an interesting response to my leaving. I asked them to send me my books. They replied that they were sorry, but my books were gone since they'd had a book burning party. I think it was their way of getting even with me for leaving.

I couldn't replace the books, but I must honestly say that, with the exception of maybe two Scripture books, I didn't miss them.

My clothes and personal belongings were put in a box and left at the Maryknoll Center House in Seoul, supposedly to be shipped home to me. They never arrived. Years later I learned that the box had been stored in the basement for years until someone decided to clear out the basement and disposed of everything. When I returned to Korea in 1989 with our two Korean daughters, there was no trace of my belongings.

I never did consider returning to the priesthood. Before my leave-of-absence was up, I petitioned Maryknoll and the Vatican to be laicized, or returned to the lay state. Having requested laicization, Maryknoll called me to headquarters where I was questioned by two priests assigned to interview any priest leaving the Society. One of the two was a classmate of mine. I didn't find him happy with my decision.

I wasn't quite sure what the interviews were all about. Perhaps it was just to ascertain that I really was making a free and honest decision. It seemed to me that the questions were more about why I had become a priest in the first place. Had I had the correct intention? Had I known what I was doing? Had I intended to remain a priest for life when I accepted ordination, etc.? It was like they were looking for a reason to say my ordination was flawed and, therefore, didn't count.

It was also somewhat like looking for a reason to grant an annulment in a marriage. I insisted that I had known what I was doing. I had entered the priesthood of my own free will. At the time I knew it was for life and I had intended it to be. Now things had drastically changed and I felt that I needed to leave. If I did not, I would probably have become either rebellious or worse—a hypocrite who lived a life he didn't believe in.

I remembered a Maryknoll priest friend of mine who had been assigned to visit parishes in the Midwest to solicit financial support and promote vocations to the priesthood. He remarked on the number of old pastors he met on his travels who had become embittered and unhappy. He felt that, if they had been committed to the life of a priest, that would not have happened. He said that he would know if he had been a good priest if he was not bitter in his old age. Many years later he was still a Maryknoll priest living in an island parish off the coast of South Korea, and he was not bitter.

During one of these visits to Maryknoll head-quarters I was standing out on the portico in front of the main building, enjoying some fresh air and reflecting on what I'd gone through that morning. Suddenly, another priest joined me. This particular man had been ordained five years before I was. I hadn't known him personally but, during the four years I lived at the Maryknoll major seminary before my ordination, I had heard about him. He had a fine reputation and was greatly admired. He was brilliant and had been sent on for further study after his ordination. I heard him speak on one occasion when he gave a short informal talk to a large gathering of faculty and students and he was very charismatic.

This priest wanted to tell me his story. He said that he had been assigned as rector at one of Maryknoll's seminaries, and had also acted as a spiritual director for some lay folk. In the process of providing spiritual direction, he fell in love with a young woman. This tore him apart. He was very much in love but, at the same time, he was committed to his celibate priesthood. The result was that he had a nervous breakdown, had to be relieved of his duties, and was sent for treatment.

Part of the therapy was shock treatment of some kind which erased some of his more recent memories. He had pretty much recovered from this treatment when a priest friend came to visit him and brought along a female friend. When the visit was over and the woman had left, he asked his priest friend who the woman was. He said she seemed familiar, but he really didn't know who she was. The priest friend told him it was the woman he had been in love with.

This priest then related how happy he felt about this. He was no longer in love. He had survived the temptation. He was still a priest. As the ordination ceremony says, "You are a priest forever." I think he must have believed that it was absolutely necessary for him to remain a priest . . . . that he had no choice. Nothing was said about whether the woman received any therapy or whatever happened to her, nor have I heard any more about him. He may have gone on to live a very productive priestly life.

I was grateful to him for sharing his story. But I couldn't tell him how I felt about his having to experience a nervous breakdown, and undergo treatment that rattled his brain and destroyed part of his memory, in order to be able to remain a priest. In one way I thought it was heroic on his part, but I considered the absolute requirement for a priest to remain celibate to be cruel and destructive. He was not allowed to love.

I knew the argument was that a priest is supposed to be in love with God. That's the goal of Christian mystics, to become one with God. But isn't human life all about love? Isn't it through love of another human being that we discover what divine love is all about? To the Vatican bureaucracy, however, priestly celibacy continues to be more important than living a life of love in a sacred marriage. Maintaining celibacy is more important than honoring love for another. Who knows what kind of holy and productive married priest this man could have been?

So, for me, this priest's story was the best argument I had ever heard for the elimination of the rule of celibacy, and the best reason I knew for leaving the priesthood. If the Vatican would not allow a married clergy, then priests should be able to leave in order to marry. I think the stories of the many priests I had known who left the active priesthood and lived remarkably dedicated lives in sacred marriages are glaring proof of this. Holiness is not limited to any particular religious status.

During the 12 years I lived in Southern California (1989-2001) prior to retirement, Louise and I were active members of the San Diego Chapter of Call to Action, a Roman Catholic reform-focused organization that has promoted the changes in the church advocated by the Vatican Council II documents.

We were also members of CORPUS, the National Organization for an Inclusive Priesthood, and came to know many wonderful married priests and their wives—whose love for God and each other could have enabled them to continue to serve the people of God, the Church, in many official ways if the hierarchy had allowed it.

CHAPTER 5

Louise

HAVING LEFT MARYKNOLL AND THE ACTIVE PRIEST-HOOD, I saw no reason to remain celibate. In thinking about marriage, I wondered about what kind of woman I would like to marry.

I had never dated in my entire life. The closest I had come to dating was attending the junior prom with a high school classmate. I found it wonderful and exciting. It also left me feeling a kind of loss. I didn't know how to talk to a girl and didn't really converse with my date much that night. Nor could I dance, and I'm sure she didn't appreciate my clumsy attempts to do so. I always had in mind my vow to become a priest, so why was I dating?

In my senior year of high school, I didn't intend to go to the prom. However, the good nuns were always after the guys, urging us to ask the girls. If the girls were going to be able to go, they needed someone to ask them. So, at the nuns' urgings, I invited the girl from our junior prom to go with me again. She politely declined since she had already accepted another boy's invitation. I was relieved. She probably was too. She was a wonderful person and I did like her. I just didn't feel I should be dating. I just wanted to get out of high school and get on with becoming a priest.

Now, here I was at age 38 wondering how to go about dating women. By now I had learned how to talk with women and feel comfortable in their presence. During that first year after leaving Maryknoll, I met many women. Although we seemed to enjoy being together, there was no strong mutual attraction. The girls I felt attracted to were not attracted to me, and I didn't feel attracted to those who were attracted to me.

How little I knew about the attractions of love. Thinking about women became a major preoccupation. I had sort of decided to avoid ex-nuns, school teachers, and nurses because I thought they would all be "too bossy." In addition, ex-nuns were too close to the religious life I had just abandoned. But I was feeling terribly lonely.

At the time I was working as a counselor in an experimental drug rehabilitation center for teenage boys in the Bronx, New York. Although stressful, it was good work. I learned a lot from the boys and from the other staff members. Work colleagues became good friends and I also had friends throughout the New York City area. But my loneliness persisted.

One Friday, when I was walking the streets of Manhattan, I remembered praying and asking God to help me meet someone with whom I could share my life. The next day Dan Charbonneau, John Hallinan, and Fred Lumen picked me up early in the morning and we drove up to Boston together to attend Bill Ahearn's wedding. All four of these men were former Maryknollers with whom I had worked in South Korea. Bill had left Maryknoll some months before me and was marrying Helen Stevens, an ex-nun he had met in Boston.

The wedding took place in the apartment of Jean Hannon, an ex-nun who had left the same religious community some time before Helen left. Dan was dating Jean at the time, even though he was living in New York City. Some weeks later they broke up and Dan later married a Korean girl who lived in New York City. Jean married a wonderful Jewish man who worked in the Boston courts and played the drums in a musical ensemble in his off hours.

During the drive up to Boston, Dan told me that, during the wedding dinner, Bill and Helen (the bridal couple) would like me to sit beside a woman who had just left the convent two weeks before. He added that she was a close friend of Helen and Jean. As I had never met Helen, Jean, or this woman, I had no objection. I really didn't give it much thought, except that it would be nice to have a conversation partner.

We arrived in Boston on time for the wedding ceremony. I didn't remember much about the wedding ceremony, except that Helen had her leg in a cast as the result of a recent skiing accident. It was a small wedding, with about fifteen people present. Almost everyone there was either an ex-nun or a former priest.

Technically, these women did not refer to themselves as ex-nuns who had left the convent. Instead, they referred to themselves as women religious who had left their community, the Daughters of Charity of St. Vincent de Paul. The other technicality was that, unlike most religious orders, Daughters of Charity did not take permanent religious vows. They renewed their vows each year on the Feast of the Annunciation.

The term "former priest" also needs some explanation. The ordination ceremony contains the words "ordained forever." Thus, the Church believes that "once a priest, always a priest." In my understanding, a "former priest" is still obligated to exercise his priesthood when there is no other priest available. Most "former" priests consider themselves to still be priests, just not active priests, even if they have been formally laicized (officially returned to the lay state).

Many "former" priests still engaged in an active ministry. Their actions were considered valid, but illicit (not approved by the hierarchy). They often officiated at weddings and funerals. Some celebrated the Eucharist within their families or in small private communities.

Certain theologians have agreed that a faith community itself can appoint a member of their own community, including selecting a woman, to preside at or celebrate a valid Eucharist (i.e., Mass). They believed this is what the early church followers did when they met to break bread in memory of what Jesus did at the Last Supper. However, the church hierarchy maintains that they are the only ones who can legitimately appoint or ordain a priest and only a priest can preside at a valid Eucharistic celebration . . . and that is the law.

Now, back to the wedding celebration! I met my dinner partner, Louise Hartnett, a tall, strikingly beautiful blonde, as we were seated for the post-wedding meal. I asked her what she intended to do now that she had left her religious community. She told me she would just continue doing what she had been doing. The only difference being that she would not be wearing religious garb. What had she been doing? She was teaching nursing students at Boston College.

While in the presence of this tall, beautiful blonde, it never occurred to me that I had told myself I wasn't interested in a relationship with a nurse, a teacher, or an ex-nun. I certainly never expected to meet someone who combined all three disqualifications. Nor was I thinking about any special relationship, or even that she was someone I would want to date. We were just having a conversation.

Bill & Helen Ahearn (Bride and Groom)
with Louise and me at their wedding.

I had enjoyed meeting Louise but, as soon as the meal was over, I put on my coat and hat. I was going out the door when Jean stopped me and asked, "Where are you going?"

I said that I had to catch the last bus back to New York which was leaving in the early afternoon.

"But we invited you for the weekend," she replied.

I explained to Jean that no one had told me this and, besides, I had no place to stay that evening. She informed me that they had a friend's apartment available upstairs in the same building for guests to use overnight. Since I really hadn't wanted to leave, I was quite happy to return to the party.

I spent the rest of the day with Louise. She suggested that she show me around Boston. It happened to be an especially cold, windy day—typical of Boston in January. I couldn't have cared less about the weather. It just felt so good walking alongside this woman. We wandered around the Prudential Center, went up to the top of the Prudential Tower, had dinner in a nice restaurant, and then went to the movies.

I didn't care what movie we saw. It just felt so good being there with Louise. I was surprised, though, at her choice of movie. Believe it or not, the movie was *Love Story*. I thought the title sounded too romantic and it did turn out to be a very sentimental film.

After the movie we returned to Jean's apartment where Louise was staying. We joined the others until it was time for me to retire to the guest apartment. Another former priest joined me there.

The next morning, I went with Louise and several of the other wedding guests to attend Mass at the Paulist Center on Boston Common. We ended up in the balcony. I remember it was especially noisy, with the children in constant motion crawling all around the altar. I liked that kind of children's participation.

After Mass we went for brunch and eventually ended up back at Jean's apartment. I just remembered that the day passed all too quickly. And this time I really did need to get to the bus station. The three men I had driven up with were all going in different directions, so I had no car ride back to New York.

I didn't want to leave Boston since I was just getting to know Louise and had no idea if I would see her again. Uncharacteristically for me (as I was slow at such things), I managed to get her telephone number. She was open to seeing me again.

I was very impressed by Louise. This ex-nun, teacher, and nurse was obviously very intelligent, very talented, very competent, very pretty, and a very poised young woman who was able to express herself very well; yet she made no attempt to act as if she was special. It was as if she didn't know all these things about herself.

Getting to know her was such a fantastic experience. She constantly amazed me. She seemed so elegant and sophisticated, yet so much herself. She didn't think of herself as sophisticated, so when someone else did and mentioned it, she would chuckle. She enjoyed the compliment, but didn't know why people saw her that way. I later learned that she was designated the "most sophisticated" in her Augusta, Maine high school class. Louise brushed off that honorific title by saying you didn't have to be all that cultured or worldly-wise to earn it in the boondocks of Maine.

Almost every weekend after that, I was on the Eastern Airlines shuttle from New York to Boston. By April, I had decided to propose and invited Louise to New York for the weekend. I had picked out a Spanish fondue restaurant in Lower Manhattan that was then all the rage, thinking this would be a good place to propose. I should have checked it out ahead of time. Much to my chagrin, the tables were only about six inches apart. If I proposed, who knows from which adjacent table an answer might come? I could have been proposing to three girls at once!

Louise & I enjoying being together, Spring 1971

I did some hard thinking during the gazpacho soup course and came up with a brilliant Plan B. We would go to the Wooden Indian Lounge for an after-dinner drink. At the lounge, we were seated right next to the Wooden Indian statue. I managed to wait until our drinks were served and then took the plunge: "Will you marry me?"

No answer! I panicked. It never occurred to me that she might say no. Suddenly I realized what a terrible mistake that was. Of course, she might! What was I to do if she said no? How should I react? What should I say? What had I done? I was frozen.

Then she smiled and said, "Yes." And at that very moment the light over the Wooden Indian statue turned on and bathed us in its light!

Louise explained later how totally surprised she was. A marriage proposal just wasn't on her mind so soon after having left her religious community. It had never occurred to me to have an engagement ring ready for her either, but Louise never said a word. She never let on that she expected anything. What a woman!

Some weeks later, we arranged to go together to pick out her engagement ring. We found one. The diamond was a little on the small side, but it was a good quality diamond in a simple platinum setting and she liked it. Then the salesperson informed me that my credit card was declined. It was maxed out and we had to charge the engagement ring to Louise's credit card.

You must be thinking by now, *"Wasn't Louise having second thoughts?"* She was, but they were all about how much money we were spending. She decided we'd do no more expensive eating out. From then on, we brown-bagged it on our weekend excursions. This was a lot less expensive and, with her, those weekends were a lot of fun.

Another characteristic of this unusual woman was that she was a natural organizer. When it came to planning and preparing for an event, like a wedding, I didn't have a clue! Planning down to the last detail was Louise's forte.

Louise found a Pierre Cardin Vogue pattern and started sewing her own wedding dress: a knee-length, ivory silk dress that was simple and beautiful. She was still adding the final touches the night before the ceremony.

She didn't tailor a suit for me, but instead took me to the original Filene's basement store in downtown Boston where we found a terrific-looking white sharkskin suit for less than 30 dollars! And, whereas I usually had to have suit jacket waistlines taken in, this one fit me perfectly. Later, when preparing to board the Swiss Air 747 at the start of our honeymoon trip, the official who body-searched me declared that it was the nicest suit he had searched all day! Later, Louise and I had a good laugh over that!

Then Louise started to plan the wedding. We drove along the New England coast north and south of Boston over several weekends looking for the right place. We found it at the White Cliffs of Plymouth, a small oceanside beach resort in Plymouth, Massachusetts. Louise wanted to be married there at dawn with the sun rising over the Atlantic Ocean.

The wedding took place on a cliff above the beach at White Cliffs on July 31, 1971, but not at dawn. It had rained buckets the day before without letup, so Louise reluctantly postponed the ceremony until 10 a.m. We were able to notify all our guests of the time change except one couple, Dick and Bea Braun. They showed up for the early ceremony at dawn only to find that no one else was there. And they left before any of us arrived at the later time. Dick and Bea thought we must have called off the wedding and we thought they hadn't come. It was months before we both learned what had really happened.

Louise arranged for a Jesuit priest friend to perform the ceremony and for another friend to do a liturgical dance. The bride had her blonde hair done in an upsweep hairdo, with yellow roses nestled in the curls, that looked especially beautiful. Much to my disappointment, Louise never repeated this upsweep hairstyle in her many different hair arrangements through the years since then.

I just kind of floated through the wedding ceremony, like it said on the Snoopy card Louise had sent me for Valentine's Day a month after we met: "My feet didn't touch the ground." Louise played her guitar and sang three songs to me during the ceremony: *We've Only Just Begun, Follow Me*, and *Since You Asked*. The last mentioned is a song written by Dan Fogelberg and recorded by Judy Collins, with the following lyrics that we both found especially meaningful.

Since You Asked

What I'll give you since you asked
is all my time together.
Take the rugged sunny days, the
warm and rocky weather.
Take the roads that
I have walked along,
Looking for tomorrow's
time, peace of mind.
As my life spills into yours,
changing with the hours,
Filling up the world with time,
turning time to flowers.
I can show you all the songs
That I never sang to
one man before.
We have seen a million stones
lying by the water,
You have climbed the hills with me
To the mountain shelter
Taken off the days one by one.
Setting them to
breathe in the sun.
Take the lilies and the lakes from
the days of childhood,
All the willow winding paths
leading up and the outward.
This is what I give. This is what I
ask you for. Nothing more.

Louise making sure my collar was in place before our wedding ceremony, with Cousin Sue looking on

We didn't invite anyone from our immediate families to the wedding, partly because of the travel distance involved and partly because we felt they might not approve of our wedding taking place over-looking a beach rather than in a church. Louise had two brothers, one who lived in Virginia and the other in California. Most of my family lived in Ohio.

My family had also invested in my ordination so I didn't think they would be all that interested in attending my wedding. I realized later that they were disappointed. My brother summed their feelings up nicely by saying, "I invited you to my wedding."

With only two exceptions, our guests were all former priests or ex-nuns. Louise invited her cousin Sue who lived in the Boston area. She came with her boyfriend and apologized for his choice of attire. He was wearing a dark pink dress jacket that Sue called his "pimp jacket." I knew the jacket. It was from a Sears store and I had bought one just like it. Later that year I wore it in Sue's company, teasing her about my "pimp jacket."

This "pimp jacket" was an example of of Louise's and my poor judgment in making clothing choices right after we'd spent almost two decades not having to make such choices—Louise wearing a blue and white habit all the time, and me the Roman collar with a black suit or cassock, except for casual wear at recreation times.

Father Joe Ciparik performing our wedding ceremony, July 31, 1971

After the wedding, a brunch was served in the resort restaurant for our guests. Louise and I were the last ones to leave, only to find that we were locked out of our Volkswagen Bug with the keys inside. I wasn't sure how that happened, but I always strongly suspected that my friend and ex-Maryknoller John Hallinan was involved. We eventually got the car door opened with the aid of a coat hanger. It was good practice because I needed to use the same technique during our honeymoon when we were parked at the site of Hitler's "Eagle's Nest" bunker in Germany. The rental car was, again, a Volkswagen Bug.

I also made some other honeymoon goofs, like losing our hotel voucher in Switzerland. This must have frustrated Louise at times, but she handled these situations with her typical aplomb. We loved Switzerland and promised ourselves we would return in ten years. We did return, but it took 25 years to do so.

After our honeymoon in Switzerland, with brief side trips to Austria and Germany, we returned to New York City and took up residence in an apartment in the Fifth Avenue Hotel in Lower Manhattan. It was a great location, but the apartment was on the second floor looking out over the roof of the hotel kitchen. We couldn't see the sky, only the walls of the rest of the building. The apartment was dark and we felt like we were living in a nice cave. However, considering our finances and how difficult it was to find decent, affordable housing in Manhattan, we felt extremely lucky to find this subsidized apartment.

Al and Louise's 1971 passport photos

Louise had left her teaching position at Boston College to follow me to New York City. She took a position teaching nursing students at Beth Israel Medical Center. John Hallinan worked there at the time and was instrumental in getting us the subsidized apartment. Louise taught at the Beth Israel School of Nursing for one year, and then did some private duty nursing before obtaining a teaching position at Lehman College in the Bronx. From our apartment in the Riverdale section of the Bronx we enjoyed a great view of the mighty Hudson River for four years.

I eventually resigned my job at the adolescent rehabilitation center and enrolled at Fordham University to earn a graduate-level certificate in school psychology. I finished the program the year New York City went into bankruptcy and no school psychology positions were available there. With the help of Louise's ex-nun friend, Marie Doyle, I was able to get work at a counseling center in the Boston area. We bought our first house in Chelmsford, Massachusetts and Louise began another stint of teaching at Boston College.

Before we left New York City, Louise had been enrolled in a doctoral program at Columbia University focused on curriculum and instruction in nursing education. She had completed her course work, but had to drive back to New York from Boston several times in order to finish and defend her doctoral dissertation, and graduate. What I remembered most about her doctoral studies was what an ordeal it was getting her thesis printed to match the requirements of the University. Word processing had just begun to be developed and Louise decided to go with that process instead of having someone type it on a manual typewriter. Getting the formatting of tables, citations, etc. done correctly using either process was extremely stressful. Louise was granted a Doctor of Education degree (EdD) in May 1980.

When we got married I had a decent job and Louise had her teaching position. We had both left religious life in our late thirties with no savings to speak of—so, we started out our life together almost penniless. This was one of the reasons we had to keep our wedding costs under control.

I had run up a small debt while looking for work and then while we were dating, but I was never really too concerned about money. My feet were still "off the ground." One thing that helped us through the

first year or two was being able to do income aver-
aging on our federal income taxes. Since we both
went from having almost zero incomes to having two
modest salaries, this brought us a healthy tax refund
to work with.

Unlike me, Louise was wise when it came to handling
money. She was careful about what she purchased. She
never wasted any food or clothes. What really amazed
me was all the energy she expended to save pennies,
but then she could turn around and purchase an expensive item if we needed it (such as a car), but only after
doing research to ascertain the best buy.

For example, she found out about the great
Swiss Air package deal that enabled us to travel to
Switzerland for our honeymoon. We had originally considered driving out to the Rocky Mountains, but Louise
knew I had loved the Heidi stories that took place in
the Swiss Alps when I was a child. So, it was easy to
talk me into honeymooning in Switzerland instead.

When it came to gambling and money matters,
Louise and I had different backgrounds and experience. I had grown up in a family in which playing
cards and poker-type games were the major enter-
tainments. And soon after we met, I introduced Louise
to handicapping horse races. Initially, she enjoyed
weighing all the variables in the *Racing Form* to figure out the best bets. But, once she realized there
were always factors beyond the bettor's knowledge
and control, she lost interest in betting on the horses.

Throughout our marriage Louise humored me
when it came to gambling. She visited horse racing
tracks and casinos with me on occasion to be socia-

ble, but she had no desire to gamble. She considered it a waste of money, while I enjoyed it and considered it legitimate entertainment. Fortunately, I never lost control and always remained a cheap bettor.

In the casinos, I liked to play the nickel video poker machines, putting in multiple nickels at a time. I would usually go with a set limit and when that was gone, I'd stop. I have gotten carried away and gone beyond that limit often enough, but my limit had always been small enough that no real harm was done. When Louise accompanied me, rather than be bored, she usually played a little video poker on a nickel machine. One day she hit a jackpot on a nickel machine and I got all excited. But she had only won $20 when I thought she should have won at least $200. Then she explained why she had only won $20: "I only put one nickel in."

It was amazing to me that nothing seemed to faze Louise. No matter how complicated or how demanding the problem, she would attack the issue and resolve it. She believed in doing whatever work came her way and doing it well. It was a matter of personal pride. I was in awe of her emotional strength.

But then, out of the blue, she would sometimes burst into tears. I would try to comfort her and stand by her, yet it just seemed so atypical. A day later she'd be back to her usual self. This didn't happen every month, but often enough that I soon caught on to how hormonal changes affected her.

As I mentioned in an earlier chapter, despite our efforts it was several years before Louise became pregnant. Our initial excitement and great joy was quickly followed by our anguish over the decision to terminate the pregnancy. I came to realize why events like this can destroy a marriage. Louise's grief and disappointment were profound. It was like she was totally wrapped up in tears and sadness. It was as if she was lost in grief and had left me. I told her that it made me feel like just walking out. This didn't lessen her sadness, but she did respond and we were able to grieve and move on together.

Besides my erroneous objections to teachers, nurses, and ex-nuns as being "too bossy", there were two qualities that I felt were extremely important for my future wife to have—to be someone I could talk with easily and to be a good mother. After spending ten years struggling to communicate in the Korean language, I knew how important it was to be able to simply talk with someone and not miss the humor, the nuances, and the unexpressed meanings, as well as clear, direct expressions of intent and feelings.

Louise was so good at saying what she felt and what she wanted. From the start, I felt that I understood her and was completely at ease and confident in her presence. I had never felt this way with any other woman.

Louise and I both wanted children. Before our marriage, I was concerned about what kind of mother Louise would be. From the start, it was evident that corporal punishment was out of the question for Louise. She just naturally related to people with care and concern. If there was a problem, she stepped back until she could deal with it.

When we adopted our girls, she was fantastic. Unlike me, she never punished them with anger. She just wanted to enjoy their growth, nourish them, and keep them happy. Of course, this wasn't always easy. No matter how nice and fair you think you are, children can be difficult. They are their own persons with their own feelings and desires.

I was amazed at what a patient, caring, and nurturing mother Louise turned out be. Perhaps I overdid my admiration for her. Was this woman a saint or was I deluding myself? I leaned toward saint, but I had to deal with her human weaknesses as well.

During our marriage, Louise taught nursing full-time in university settings for 32 years. After retiring from the University of San Diego in 2003, she returned to hands-on nursing care as an RN Case Manager at Nathan Adelson Hospice in the Las Vegas valley three days a week for seven and a half years. It can be very stressful work, but she really cared about her patients and did everything she could to make their last days as comfortable as possible. Louise enjoyed job-sharing with another nurse who was about the same age. They cared for the same caseload of patients and dubbed themselves "the Golden Girls of Nathan Adelson Hospice."

I had been after Louise for years to fully retire. She had promised and even set dates to do so, but each date would come and go and she would still be working. She gave three reasons for this: she found the work especially satisfying, liked the extra income, and felt she was making a real difference in the lives of the patients for whom she was responsible. When Louise finally retired in September 2011, she was 77 years old.

But about that human side: Louise sometimes came home from work looking frazzled and started taking it out on me. I'd been home all day doing nothing very important, so I couldn't complain if she wanted to dump some anger or frustration on me. Most of the time she just wanted me to listen and understand when she'd had a frustrating day. But there were times when it got to me. That's when I'd remind "Miss Crabby" that I hadn't done anything to upset her. This was usually enough to get her to back off and, hopefully, find some humor in the situation.

Another big issue for me was her reluctance to be totally upfront with me about her plans ahead of time. She might have had a whole list of things she wanted to do that involved me, but she would only tell me the first one. For example, she would have me go shopping with her and I'd be expecting to finish one shopping chore and go home. But she'd add another, then another, and then one more. By this time, "Mr. Crabby" (me) would be in a rage. I just needed her to tell me her itinerary ahead of time so that I knew what I was getting into. We've had some serious battles over that particular habit.

Obstacles and problems bothered Louise, just as they do anyone else, but she attacked problems the same way she shopped—resolved to work out a worthy solution. People problems, whether at home or at work, worried her but she didn't get angry. She worried about each problem until she was able to work out a solution that respected each person and was fair to all involved.

Throughout fifty years of marriage we had some serious disagreements, but nothing we weren't able to work out. Our political, religious, psychological, and parental beliefs complemented each other and helped us to grow together. For example, we have either walked out of a church together, or sworn never to attend a particular church again, because of what we each considered offensive remarks from the celebrant concerning abortion, the Pope, or other religious issues. Politically, we almost always voted the same. The occasional difference was when Louise favored a particular woman candidate.

CHAPTER 6

Ann and Lisa

D URING THE 1980-81 SCHOOL YEAR, LOUISE WAS awarded a Robert Wood Johnson Nurse Faculty Fellowship in Primary Care at the University of Maryland. During that year, we moved to Baltimore and she completed their Adult Nurse Practitioner Program.

Soon after moving there, we received a mailer advertising a six-week course on "Family Building Through Adoption" to be held at Loyola University and sponsored by Catholic Charities. Loyola University was just a couple of blocks from the apartment building where we were living.

We had previously thought about adoption, but had not followed up on it. So, we decided to attend the classes, get the information, and finally decide one way or the other.

The first class was very interesting. It was all about the necessity of giving up your "dream child." I hadn't thought about adoption in those terms. It made me realize that I, indeed, had fostered a biological dream child in the back of my mind. To be in the right frame of mind for adopting, we had to give up the need to continue our lives and posterity only through biological children. The important thing was to give up our dream children and focus on the real children we would adopt. It made a lot of sense.

During the next few classes, a parade of adoptive parents and adoptees who were now adults shared their stories—their lived experiences as adoptive parents and adoptees. We also heard about issues concerning adoption from a doctor and a lawyer.

Then came the shocker: a female special education teacher who was single and blind told us about the children she had adopted. One was blind, one was physically handicapped, one had Down's Syndrome, and there were two more adoptees also handicapped in some way. One was a baby still on infant formula. The woman only had help from her mother, who was over 90 years of age but could see to measure the infant formula. The amazing thing was that this woman didn't act as if she thought she was doing anything extraordinary. She made it sound like she had an ordinary family.

How did she cope? Louise and I wondered. The word "cope" didn't seem to be in her vocabulary. She wasn't coping. She was just living with her family and dealing with ordinary difficulties that came up. Wow! If this blind woman could parent so well with a family like that, how could we shrink from adoption for fear of not being up to the task?

THE ADOPTION PROCESS

We decided to apply for an adoption, did the paperwork, and were deemed qualified to adopt. Being older, we felt we should adopt older children. Also, because of Louise's demanding work, we didn't feel we could adopt and care for an infant.

Although Catholic Charities told us about several international adoption agencies, we thought we should first concern ourselves with the possible adoption of American children. The first potential adoptees to become available were from a family of five children ranging in age from four to fourteen. Being naïve, and having no idea how hard and costly it would be to take on such a large instant family, we said, "Why not?" However, the children were quickly adopted by someone outside the State of Maryland.

That gave us pause. It seemed that, if we didn't feel able to provide a home for hard-to-adopt American children with special needs, we were in for a long wait. So, we decided to try an international adoption from South Korea. Having lived and worked in South Korea for ten years, I was familiar with the culture and language and admired the Korean people very much. Again, "Why not try?"

Catholic Charities in Baltimore did not have a license to arrange international adoptions, but they worked cooperatively with agencies that did. We were connected with the "Friends of the Children of Vietnam," an agency in Colorado that handled Asian overseas adoptions.

Within a month or so we were told about two "neat" young Korean girls, ages eleven and six, who had recently been placed for adoption. The agency sent us a picture of the two beautiful girls named Hyang Joon and Hei Ran, and we joyfully said, "Yes."

The adoption process involved multiple requirements. In some ways, the waiting time involved can be compared to the nine months of a pregnancy. You wait and hope all is going well, and that there will not be any last-minute foul-ups.

As part of the adoption process the girls spent a short time in an orphanage in Seoul run by Al's seminary classmate, former Maryknoll missionary colleague, and friend, Father Ben Zweber. We learned that they had been placed for adoption there by aging grandparents in their extended Korean Catholic family. Their grandparents had cared for the girls during the past several years since their father had died and their mother had left them behind. Their grandparents' health was failing and they wanted to be sure the girls would have a bright future in America.

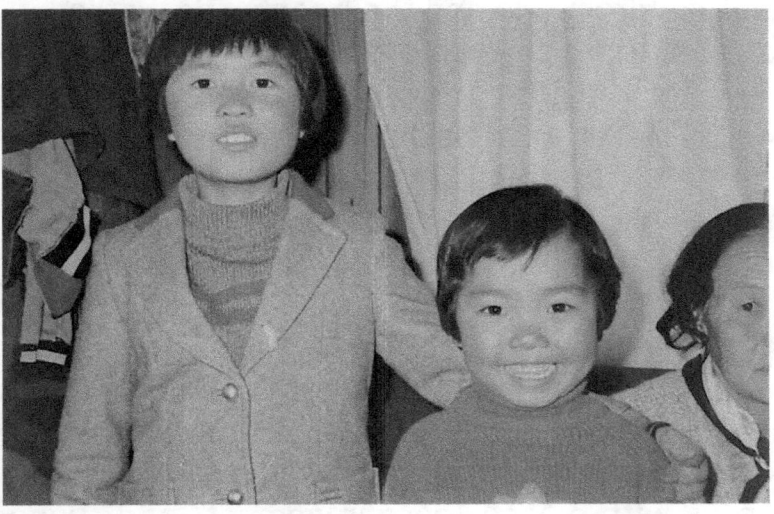

Hyang Joon (Ann) and Hei Ran (Lisa) in Korea prior to their adoption

At last, we got the long-awaited news that the girls would arrive in the United States around the end of July or early August 1981. This was perfect since Louise's Fellowship would be ending on the first of August.

There were fees and airfare for a chaperone, etc. to be paid, all amounting to about $4,000. Louise and I were living on a tight budget, but things do work out. My mother had died in February 1981. She was anything but rich and her estate was divided equally between five children. My share of the inheritance from my mother, however, enabled us to pay these costs. We were sorry that my mother never had the opportunity to meet the girls.

The woman running the Catholic Charities Adoption Program was a Mormon. She had volunteered to run the program and promised Catholic Charities that she would earn her own salary. She and her husband had adopted several children and they were committed to finding good homes for other children. She and the people she worked with were terrific. She even did a follow-up visit with us a few months after the girls arrived when we were living in Beverly, Massachusetts.

One of the things this woman did was organize parents who were about to adopt into groups. We met with three other couples and dialogued about why we were adopting, our expectations, the wait, and the demands to be met. The idea was to form a like-minded group with whom we could share our experiences after adoption and not feel alone. There would be other adoptive parents to help us with advice, encouragement, and support.

This group was helpful to us prior to the adoption. Unfortunately, since we left Baltimore so soon after the girls' arrival, our membership in this adoptive parents' group was short-lived.

OUR NEW DAUGHTERS' ARRIVAL

The girls' arrival date was going to be perfect— or so we thought. Louise's fellowship year was coming to a close at the end of July and we were then scheduled to return to Massachusetts where we had purchased a house. We thought we'd be moved back to Massachusetts and settled in our new home before the girls arrived.

Our best laid plans had to change when we received word that the girls would be arriving at Kennedy International Airport in New York on the evening of July 16, 1981. We drove our Volkswagen Rabbit to John Hallinan's house in Queens. John, a former Maryknoll colleague of mine in South Korea, and Maria, his beautiful Korean wife, took us out to Kennedy Airport to meet our two girls. Just like that, we became instant parents! I could hardly believe it, but I also couldn't help but wonder what these two little girls were feeling.

When they arrived, each was carrying a small backpack. They had no other belongings but the clothes on their backs. They were both very skinny and looked frightened. Everything was new to them, including these strange-looking people who were going to be their new parents.

The younger, Hei Ran (Lisa) was six and a half years old. She came willingly into my arms. Eleven-year-old Hyang Joon (Ann) took Louise's hand. Maria talked to them in Korean and we set off to return to John and Maria's home.

John and Maria were able to communicate verbally with the girls while Louise and I were mostly limited to nonverbal communication with them. John was American, but he was fluent in Korean. Maria was Korean, but she also spoke some English. Their two daughters, Jennifer and Monique, grew up speaking both languages. At first, they didn't even distinguish between the two languages. We discovered that our new daughters only knew the ABC's and how to say "Mommy" and "Daddy" in English.

Ann and Lisa were very tired after their long journey. They ate a little and soon went to sleep. It helped a lot that the girls' first experience of America was in this Korean-speaking household with other children. Everything didn't feel so strange to them there.

The next morning, we drove to Baltimore in our Volkswagen Rabbit with the girls sleeping in the back seat. Our Baltimore apartment was on the fourth floor and already had packing boxes scattered around.

That first evening with our new daughters was horrendous. Ann refused to eat and started crying. She demanded that she be returned to her grandmother. She said they were promised that they could return home to Korea if they didn't like it here. Louise couldn't understand Korean, but she certainly understood the crying.

Ann put on her backpack, insisted that she and her sister were going back to Korea, and told Lisa to put on her backpack. Lisa looked at her sister, then at us, and then they went out the door and down the hall. I followed. Fortunately, Ann didn't know how to use the elevator, so they had to return to our apartment.

The crying continued. Louise and I were near tears ourselves. Ann sounded so broken-hearted and absolutely miserable. We felt the same way. I kept thinking, *What have we done? Maybe this was a mistake.*

Louise and I felt so helpless, and didn't know what to do to help Ann feel better. Lisa appeared to be settling in with us, yet she was sticking by her sister. We explained that we couldn't take them back, but Ann could certainly write a letter to her grandmother in South Korea.

No! Ann wanted to go back. The crying and wailing continued. It wasn't just ordinary crying—it was gut-wrenching and there was no let-up. Finally, I told Ann that she could continue to cry if she wanted to, but we were very tired of listening to her. I led her into the bedroom and told her she was to stay there until she stopped crying. Then she could come back out and join us in the living room. To my surprise, it worked. She cried for maybe ten minutes more and then she stopped and came out into the living room.

Ann did write a letter to her grandmother. I didn't read it, but promised to send it. Our correspondence was not sent directly to her grandmother and other relatives in South Korea, but was routed through The Friends of the Children of Vietnam agency in

Colorado. I doubted that they ever forwarded the letter to the girls' grandmother in South Korea.

The crying ended, but Ann still refused to eat or drink. Louise was really concerned, fearful that she might have to take Ann to the hospital if she continued her fast and became dehydrated. This would have added to the trauma of her separation from her Korean family and her arrival in a foreign country and culture.

That first night Ann and Lisa slept on the floor in our bedroom in sleeping bags. I knew that in South Korea it was not unusual for everyone living in the rural areas to sleep in the same room on their heated ondol floor. Actually, the girls were afraid to sleep in a room by themselves that night. A long time after that Ann confessed the reason why she stopped crying and returned to the living room: she was afraid of ghosts when she was in the bedroom by herself.

The next morning, we found that Ann had disappeared! We were stunned by this turn of events until Louise looked out the window and saw her picking berries off a bush on the apartment house grounds below. Later, Lisa liked to pick flowers from the neighbors' front yards in Beverly, Massachusetts as she walked by. That was one thing the girls had to learn—not to pick things from other people's properties.

That morning, Ann watched Louise fix pancakes for breakfast and, much to Louise's relief, she decided to try the food since she'd watched it being prepared. Overall, the girls didn't have too much trouble adapting to American food. Their diet in South Korea had been unvaried, consisting mainly of rice and kim chi. Considering how skinny they were, they certainly had not been eating enough. It turned out that they liked the variety in the American diet and have continued to like to try new restaurants and new kinds of food. Over the years, they often got Louise and I to try new dishes.

*Al with Lisa and Ann in our Baltimore
apartment soon after their arrival in the U.S.*

There were some real culinary surprises for them those first days in America. For example, ketchup and spaghetti sauce looked to them like Korean hot red pepper sauce. They were very surprised by their first non-spicy tastings of these foods. Louise gave Ann her first banana. It quickly disappeared and

Louise was happy because she thought she'd found something Ann liked. It was only sometime later that Ann confessed she had stuffed the banana down the garbage disposal when Louise wasn't looking.

The girls soon discovered that the apartment complex had a swimming pool. They couldn't swim, but they were eager to try it. Luckily, a friend who lived in the apartment complex took on the task of watching over them at the pool. The other residents at the pool welcomed the girls and enjoyed watching their excitement. This was a great plus, because time at the pool kept the girls occupied while Louise and I continued to pack and get ready for our move back to Massachusetts.

The immediate crisis with Ann was over, but it was still like walking on eggshells for the next seven months. That time period was very trying. I knew it was to be expected, but knowing this didn't make it any easier. At the time, it felt like Ann's resistance would never end—like we were going to have to put up with this acting out forever.

The fact that Lisa didn't act out then didn't mean she wouldn't in the future. For the time being, she just wanted to settle down with her new mommy and daddy and get on with it. I figured we'd be in for it in her teen years. Fortunately, that gave us an almost ten-year reprieve.

SETTLING DOWN WITH OUR NEW FAMILY

By the end of July 1981, we had loaded all our goods into a large U-Haul truck. Louise's teenage niece, Donna Hartnett, came up from Virginia to help watch the girls during our journey back to Massachusetts. I drove the U-Haul and led the way with Donna and Lisa as passengers. Louise drove the Volkwagen Rabbit with Ann.

When we reached New Jersey, I decided it was time for a rest stop and took the next highway exit. Much to my consternation, Louise drove right on by—not seeing that the U-Haul truck she was following had turned off the freeway. Actually, she was exhausted from the emotional demands of the girls, as well as finishing up the packing and getting on the road. I had to drive right through the rest stop and chase after her on the highway.

Late that night we arrived in Andover, Massachusetts and stayed at the home of Joe and Gail Baggot, since the house we had purchased in Beverly would not be available until late the next morning. Joe was also a former Maryknoller who had worked several years in East Africa before leaving Maryknoll and then marrying Gail.

Joe worked at the same counseling center in Lawrence where I had worked before spending the year in Baltimore. He and Gail were among our best friends in the Boston area. Gail made great Irish soda bread and loved to go shopping. Joe was a natural storyteller with a great sense of humor. As he aged, he grew a belly and a beard and looked like a dead ringer for Santa Claus.

The next morning, we drove to Beverly and began moving into our new home. The house had a large yard where Lisa found all sorts of small wildflowers to pick. As city residents we had access to an ocean beach within walking distance. Donna took the girls to the beach while we began unpacking. The girls loved that beach and spent a lot of time swimming and collecting sand dollars there that August.

Our split-level house was big enough for the girls to have their own bedrooms, but they weren't too interested in that at first. For the rest of the summer, they continued to sleep on the floor beside our bed.

When it came time for school, we suggested that it was time for them to move to their own rooms. Lisa took it as a measure of growing up. She agreed that it was time to sleep in her own room if she was going to school. And, always one to speak frankly, she declared: "This way I won't have to hear dad fart." If Lisa was up to it, then Ann had to be as well, despite the possibility of ghosts. But Ann slept with the shade up because the light from the nearby streetlight was a major comfort.

The local public school was terrific in taking responsibility for teaching the girls English. Lisa had never attended school in South Korea and entered first grade. Ann had done well in her Korean school, so she was placed in the fifth grade. Math was the one subject Ann immediately had no trouble with because she could work out the problems in her head in Korean.

Mastering the English language was their major task. I knew they would be good at learning the language because they both had good ears for music. In South Korea I had seen firsthand that Maryknollers who were good in music had a good ear for linguistic sounds and mastered the Korean language easily.

I did not have a good ear for music and the Korean language was a constant frustration for me. I did eventually learn to communicate fairly well, but never lost my American accent. I also tended to express things in "Americanese" (that is, not as Koreans expressed their thoughts). In the Korean language there is one form used for adults and a different form used with children. I had only learned the adult form. So Ann and Lisa got a kick out of my using the adult form of their language when communicating with them, since in South Korea they had only been spoken to in the children's form.

Once, during the first weeks the girls were with us, Bill Ahearn telephoned and talked with them in Korean. They marveled at how well he could speak their language. Louise mentioned to them that I also spoke Korean. The girls agreed, but said that Bill's Korean was "not like Daddy's."

The best thing the elementary school did was hiring someone to spend an hour a day with each girl teaching them English. Mrs. Nack was very good at this and Ann and Lisa learned a lot from her. They still remember how much they liked her.

Along about March 1982 Louise and I thought Lisa would be ready to move into the second grade the following Fall, so I asked Lisa's first grade teacher about this. To our surprise, the teacher said she didn't think so. By then Lisa was speaking English very well at home and seemed to be very smart.

Our New Family, Fall 1981

A month later we met with the teacher again, intending to tell her we still thought Lisa should advance to second grade. Before I could say anything, the teacher told us she had changed her mind. All of a sudden, Lisa had blossomed and was participating in class a lot more. Louise and I were delighted to hear this. It reminded us that we had been very amused at hearing Lisa, standing on our rear deck, loudly imitating her teacher:

"Debbie, I said sit down. Quiet John! Stop talking!"

PARENTING LESSONS LEARNED

After one year in America, English was no longer a problem for the girls. We teased Ann a bit because it took a lot of practice for her to pronounce certain words like "aurora" correctly because there is no hard "r" sound in Korean. But she was determined and one day proudly demonstrated that she could pronounce those kinds of words correctly.

Personality-wise, Lisa was always confident, eager, and ready to try whatever. Ann's attitude and behavior, though, were still problematic. There were times when she seemed happy and bubbly and was a real joy to be around. But it didn't take much to set her off.

One night an especially difficult situation occurred. Louise had begun teaching at the University of Lowell. Her commute involved an 80-mile round trip drive each day. This particular day Louise returned from work, fixed dinner, and then took Ann shopping at the mall for some special items needed for school.

When they returned, Ann came storming into the house and went immediately to her room, slamming the door. Louise followed looking very upset. Louise told me how angry she was. After the long day at work, returning to fix dinner, then taking Ann shopping to get her some special things she needed for school, this was the thanks she got for all of her efforts.

"What happened?" I asked.

Louise said that, when they were going through the store checkout, Ann asked for some gum. Louise said "No" to the sugared gum because she didn't want the girls to get in the habit of pleading for junk every time they saw that stuff at the checkout. When Ann heard the "No" she got angry. All the way home her anger escalated.

When they arrived home, Ann was raging and Louise was furious. I told Louise that all she needed to do was to go in and give Ann a good hug. Louise said there was no way she could do that. She was just too angry.

"Okay," I said, "I'll do it." I entered Ann's room to find her desk turned upside down and the room looking like a wreck. Ann was crying. I grabbed her, shook her, and pushed her onto the bed telling her to "Stop it!"

Of course, that didn't happen. Then I caught myself. I knew my response was wrong. I apologized and told Ann we loved her, but the weeping and wailing continued. She kept calling for her grandmother in Korean.

My words couldn't make up for my angry outburst, so I decided I should just leave her room. I opened the door to leave and there was Louise, ready to come in. She told me she was okay now.

I left and Louise laid down beside Ann on the bed, hugged her, and talked softly to her. Ann continued crying for her grandmother in Korean for several more minutes. Then, suddenly, everything changed. I was standing outside the closed door listening when Ann turned to Louise and I heard her say in English, "I'm sorry, mommy. I'm sorry."

I was thrilled and deeply touched. Ann had bonded with Louise. It was going to be all right. This happened in October. It would be months more before Ann bonded with me.

Our parenting philosophy was basically very simple. I was raised in a German Catholic family where misbehavior was dealt with physically. It didn't happen often, but disobedience could be met with slaps or spanking or the threats of such. I grew up thinking this punitive approach was how all kids were raised. After all, I'd turned out okay, hadn't I? It had seemed unbelievable to me later on when a fellow Maryknoller told me his parents had never laid a hand on him.

It took me years of study in psychology and professional counseling experience to learn that the punitive approach did not work well. I especially learned from my own experience of being unable to deal in a constructive manner with behavior problems and children acting out. I discovered that, in this respect, I had not turned out okay. My reaction to Ann in this instance was a good example. If caught off guard, my immediate reaction was to punish. I would quickly realize I was wrong and recover, but by then the damage was done. My punitive behavior was worse than Ann's acting out behavior.

Ann had good reason to be angry. It wasn't just Louise's denial of the gum. To Ann, Louise's "No" was felt as rejection. She had lost her father due to a tragic death. For emotional, economic, and cultural reasons, she had also lost her mother. Then she lost her grandparents and other relatives, as well as her friends, when she was put in an orphanage in South Korea. And then she was sent to America.

An observer might think she should have felt lucky to be sent to America. However, from her perspective, she had lost her family, country, culture, and language and was forced to live with these strange Americans. It was just one rejection, one loss after another for this eleven-year-old to endure. That rejection was what Ann had felt when Louise said "No." This situation also came at a time when Louise and Ann's verbal communication was still problematic.

In returning to Ann's room to straighten it up, I discovered that, even though it looked chaotic, nothing had really been damaged except a picture of Ann, herself, which she had torn up. This indicated to me that she didn't like herself and was feeling that something must be wrong with her to have earned all of this misfortune and rejection.

Yes, she had good reason to be angry. Of course, her anger got dumped back on us who then felt unappreciated for all we were trying to do for her. Actually, if we really wanted to love Ann, this was the time to practice the second agreement from Don Miguel Ruiz's book, *The Four Agreements*: "Don't take things personally." Patience and love were what were called for.

Our second parenting rule was to never punish someone for expressing a negative feeling. We all love to hear our children tell us that they love us. But, in the course of any human relationship, there are times when we have positive feelings and there are times when we have negative feelings. For example, "I hate you." is a common reaction when children are denied something they want. We tried to simply accept Ann's and Lisa's negative reactions and suggest more constructive ways to act.

Feelings are neither good nor bad. They just are. The way we react to our feelings can be good or bad, constructive or destructive. For example, if I feel hate toward someone it is good to talk with that person about why and work on developing a positive relationship that will dissolve the hatred.

Physical restraint is appropriate when a child's behavior is threatening harm to himself or herself or to others, but punishment is not. Actually, this applies to most adult behavior as well.

When growing up I was not allowed to express negative feelings and didn't even know that I had them. I didn't want that to happen to our girls. If they said they hated me that was okay. I accepted it.

FUN TIMES WITH THE GIRLS

There were some very good times with the girls that first year. It wasn't all acting out. For example, Ann and Lisa had never experienced Halloween in South Korea. Louise dressed Ann as a princess and Lisa as Casper, the Friendly Ghost, and went out trick-or-treating with them. They returned, all excited, showing us all the candy people had given them. One man even gave them some change because he had no candy. They couldn't believe people gave them candy just for the asking.

The girls' birthdays in South Korea had been celebrated mainly by giving them a special treat, like a bowl of strawberries. For Lisa's seventh birthday on December 5, 1981 we had a birthday party for her and invited some of her classmates. Before the party, it was touchy going. I asked Ann to help with the preparations, but she ran off to her room and didn't come out until the party was over. Lisa couldn't understand why we were giving party favors away to her guests when she didn't have those things herself. She felt much better about this after she opened all the birthday gifts her friends brought to the party, as well as those from Louise and me.

That first Fall we brought Ann and Lisa to a Korean school in Concord, Massachusetts on Saturday mornings. The purpose of this school was to help Korean children learn or retain their knowledge of the Korean language and culture. Ann and Lisa enjoyed the activities there to some extent, but didn't want to continue going there in the new year. One day a Mrs. Kim saw Ann in a local grocery store. She introduced herself, and thereafter provided the girls with some connection to their Korean heritage.

Like Halloween, Christmas—as celebrated in the United States—was also outside of the girls' experience. We told Ann that we would match the amount she saved from her weekly allowance so she could do some Christmas shopping. She had about twenty dollars when Louise took her shopping for gifts for the family and her teachers. Ann came back all upset and carried on about how mom made her spend all her money buying things for others and she hadn't gotten one thing for herself. To Ann, who had never had any money before, twenty dollars was an immense sum.

That first Christmas morning helped Ann to understand the giving and receiving spirit of the holidays. The girls still remember how exciting it was to open all the presents. Even though the gifts of a doll house and some games, etc. were modest by American standards, Ann and Lisa had never experienced anything like that before.

Another memorable event took place on New Year's Eve. Louise and I were invited to a New Year's Eve party at a friend's condominium on the Charles River in Boston. We arranged for a babysitter so we could attend. Prior to this we had never gone anywhere without taking the girls with us. We explained to them that children were not invited to the party, and that the babysitter would be there so they wouldn't be alone. And we told them we'd be home by midnight. The babysitter came and was prepared to play with the girls. Lisa took her up on that immediately, but Ann went to her room and closed the door.

We returned at 12:15 a.m. and when the garage door opened there was Ann, hands on her hips, pointing her finger and angrily reproving us: "You said 12 o'clock!" Then she ran off to her room.

We couldn't help but laugh. I said to Louise, "I guess she missed us!"

I had learned that behavioral improvement needed to be measured in small increments with our adopted children. To me, Ann's behavior in this instance was really positive. She was expressing her anger at being left behind and our not returning at the exact time we said we'd be home. It meant that she was still afraid of being abandoned again. After all, she wasn't worth keeping, was she? Now that we were home and hadn't left her for good, she was reassured about her worth.

We gave both girls a small allowance each week and every Sunday morning they walked together down the street to the neighborhood store, bought the Sunday paper for us, and picked out some candy for themselves. The store proprietor enjoyed their visits and gave them some extra treats.

As mentioned before, both girls loved living near the local beaches. During Summer 1982 Lisa entered a contest run by the local recreation department and was crowned Miss Dane Street Beach!

In February 1982 Ann had a truly great insight, an epiphany. Her relationship with Louise had been positive ever since the previous October. It was different with me. It didn't take much for her to get angry with me. Her eyes would blaze and she would say she hated me. She'd put all the emotion she could behind those words. She meant it.

I didn't remember what specific situations caused Ann's anger, but I responded the way I usually did. I would say I was concerned that she felt that way and that I didn't hate her. I would tell her that we loved her and thought she was someone special.

To my surprise, on this occasion she replied, "Why don't you hate me?" I responded, "We have no reason to hate you." I repeated that we loved her and thought she was special. Then I asked her, "Do you want me to hate you?"

"Yes." she replied. That ended the confrontation and she walked away. However, she had changed.

Many times after that Ann became angry with me, but she was never again able to feel the depth of emotion she had felt before. She had said, "Yes." She had expressed out loud that she expected us to hate her. That is what she thought she deserved. Now she began to believe that we really did love her and weren't about to throw her away. She began to accept her worth.

RETURN TO CHURCH ATTENDANCE

After I left Maryknoll and the priesthood, I continued to attend Mass regularly. But after a few months I realized that each time I left a church after Mass I was feeling angrier than when I entered it. This wasn't right. I still hadn't come to terms with my anger at the Roman Catholic Church's resistance to change and, therefore, my need to leave the priesthood. So, I stopped going to church.

For me this was a major decision. I didn't feel that I had lost my faith, but I certainly stopped practicing it. I must have been deeply angry to convince myself to abandon attendance at Sunday Mass and reception of the Eucharist. Throughout the first ten years of our marriage Louise and I seldom attended

Mass. Louise joined me in taking a break from a strict religious practice.

But then, having formed a family with the two girls, we felt that we should give our children a religious base. The adoption agency told us that a Catholic family had been suggested for the girls because their Korean family was Catholic. (This turned out to be true. We later discovered that her uncle had been the Korean tutor for Father Al Fleming many years before.)

The girls talked about attending Catholic catechism classes in South Korea, but neither girl had been baptized. So, we returned to attending church on a regular basis and had Ann and Lisa prepare for baptism, be baptized, and then receive their First Communion. By that time, I had resolved most of my anger toward the Church and again began to feel at home there.

At first, both Lisa and Ann were at peace with attending Mass and learning about their religion. It was about eight years later when Lisa rebelled. She cried and carried on that she did not believe in God and didn't want to be forced to attend church. It wasn't a passing fad with her, but something she felt deeply. Both Louise and I felt it was wrong to force religion on her. We had to rely on our example; but more importantly, we knew that God would not abandon her. We entrusted Lisa to God's care. Ann has continued to practice her Catholic faith and attends weekly Mass to this day.

Louise and I had met many Catholic parents with similar experiences. Their children were baptized and raised in the Catholic faith. But they no longer attended church, claiming that the Catholic faith, teachings, and rules and regulations were no longer meaningful to them. Our generation was born and raised Catholic and never really considered that we had a choice. Today it seems that most Catholic children need to experience a personal faith encounter of some kind. Just being raised in a Catholic family is not enough.

I had a mixed reaction to this phenomenon. It saddened me because I realized that faith in God had been such a source of strength in my own life. I firmly believed my life would have been a disaster without it. (And some people may consider my life to have been a disaster anyway.) During the years I wasn't practicing my religion, I believe that I experienced an inner conversion. And this inner conversion enabled me to then practice my religion in a real way, not just going through the motions. I also knew that many people who don't attend church are still living very good and meaningful lives. They have not lost their values or their sense of morality.

In 1983 we moved into a townhouse condominium in North Chelmsford, Massachusetts which was a lot closer to Louise's work. We lived there for a couple of years before moving to Wisconsin. During that time, Ann and Lisa became United States citizens in a ceremony at the courthouse in Lowell.

Al and the girls on the day they became US citizens

The girls enjoyed the swimming pool at the complex and one day Lisa was lucky enough to dive down and bring up treasure—a five or ten dollar bill! Ann started participating in the local "Y" swim team and her willingness to get up at the crack of dawn for swim practice before school amazed us.

Each girl had gotten a pet hamster while we lived in Beverly. One night, when I was sound asleep in our bedroom on the second floor of our North Chelmsford townhouse, I was awakened by the sensation of little prickly feet crawling over my forehead. Lisa's hamster, Squeaky, had clawed himself all the way up the carpeted stairs and onto the bed. Now that's perseverance for you!

Unfortunately, the little fellow was gasping his last breaths a few months later. We had to rush him to the vet for Lisa's sake, even though there was no real hope for his survival! Needless to say, he was given the pet version of a state funeral and burial!

During the two summers we lived in North Chelmsford, Louise worked as a camp nurse at Forest Acres Camp in Fryeburg, Maine. We could never have afforded to send the girls to such an upscale camp, but their attendance there was free because of Louise's position as camp nurse. This gave them the opportunity to participate in a variety of camp activities like swimming, horseback riding, hiking, golf, other sports, and creative arts, as well as enjoying field trips to ocean beaches and the like.

OUR MOVE TO OSHKOSH, WISCONSIN

We expected to live in our North Chelmsford townhome for the foreseeable future when, out of the blue, a call came for Louise from the Dean of the University of Wisconsin-Oshkosh (UWO) School of Nursing. She was trying to recruit a new Associate Dean for the school and wanted Louise to come for an interview.

Louise felt that she should at least explore this career opportunity, so off she flew to Oshkosh, Wisconsin. And we were soon involved in the process of selling our townhouse, traveling to Oshkosh to find a place to live, packing everything up, and moving in time for Louise to start her new position and the girls to start school there in Fall 1985.

I was fortunate to get a job as a minority student advisor in the admissions office at UWO—one of the best jobs I ever had. Lisa started the 5th grade and Ann was enrolled in middle school.

It took us a while to get used to the differences in culture between New England and Wisconsin. For example, after church one freezing cold Sunday that first winter we stopped off at an ice fishing event by Lake Winnebago. We were surrounded by folks in skimobile outfits ingesting bratwursts and beer in tents while frozen fish were strung up all over the place. The little shacks of the fishermen were scattered over the frozen lake.

Another example of culture shock was Lisa having to get an extra pair of sneakers that were only to be worn in the gym at school to help preserve the gym floor. During music performances at her middle school Ann was the only child with black hair on the stage—a sharp contrast to the blonde children of mainly northern European descent. Ann and Lisa experienced occasional racial bias in Oshkosh, but nothing really traumatic.

The difference in winter climate between Wisconsin and Massachusetts was demonstrated by the fact that, in Oshkosh winters, people had to use special electric blankets to prevent their car engines from freezing overnight and ensure that their car would start in the morning. Louise recognized that it was a different degree of winter cold when her legs ached just walking from the adjacent parking lot into the school of nursing building.

In May we were introduced to the lake flies that hatched from the lake each year. They didn't bite but flew in green swarms that stained anything they touched. Many houses near the lake were painted the same sickly green color so lake fly stains wouldn't be apparent. We even heard about people running fans inside their homes that faced toward the door so the breeze created would prevent swarms of the lake flies from entering the house when the door was opened.

ANN AND LISA GROW UP

Ann and Lisa were personality opposites in many ways. One example was the way they responded to commands. If I told Ann to do something, she would often object but then go and do it. Lisa would agree to do whatever was asked, but then not do it. One summer morning I told Lisa she had to clean her room. She said she would. In the afternoon, I told her again. Later, I reminded Lisa that she still had not cleaned her room. Again, she assured me that she would.

Sometime after dinner, when Lisa was watching TV, I turned the TV off and told her, "Go clean your room now." Lisa immediately burst into tears, crossed the room and tramped up the stairs.

Halfway up she stopped, turned, and with tears streaming down her face said, "Dad, you're a fucking asshole."

I was stunned. We didn't say things like that. If she had been standing beside me, I probably would have automatically slapped her face. That would have been the wrong thing to do and I was grateful that she was not standing next to me at that moment. I said the only thing I could think of to say: "That may be so, but you still have to clean your room." And Lisa did.

I had been invited to talk about adoption at a local business gathering the next day at noon. As I was going out the door, Lisa came running up to ask me what I was going to talk about. I told her that I was going to talk about "you girls" and that I guessed I had to tell them my daughter thought I was a "fucking asshole."

Her head dropped and she was silent for a minute. Then she said, "I'm sorry, Dad. I'll never say that again." She's been angry with me many times since then, but she's never repeated those words.

Ann wanted to continue swimming after our move to Wisconsin. She first joined the local "Y" swim team. Practice was scheduled every day at 6:30 a.m. before school and Ann was expected to put in many grueling laps. I didn't expect her to last; but learned that, when Ann set out to do something, she persevered. She ended up swimming distance events that were especially grueling.

By the time she started high school, Ann easily made the swim team. She was a not great swimmer, but she had practiced so hard that by then she had an advantage over anyone just joining the team. Lisa followed her sister and swam with the "Y" team until she got to high school. Then she stopped.

Louise and I drove around Wisconsin many winter weekends bringing the girls to their swim meets. We spent many hours socializing with other parents in the very warm, humid indoor pool areas watching our children compete. Then we drove home in the dark on the snowy, icy roads.

Lisa and Ann were both good in music. Early on, Ann loved to sing when we were traveling in the Volkswagen Rabbit. She was used to singing as loud as she could in the outside courtyard at her Korean school. That was how she wanted to sing in our car. I kept asking her to tone it down because it hurt my ears. She took that to mean that I didn't like her singing and eventually she stopped. Years later she still laughingly blamed me for no longer singing.

Ann took up the clarinet and played in the high school band. At Christmastime Louise, Lisa and I watched Ann playing her clarinet in an Oshkosh Christmas parade, freezing her bare fingers! She never touched a clarinet after high school.

Lisa took piano lessons for a short time and Louise took lessons with the same teacher. Louise had always felt deprived because she had not had this opportunity when she was a child. She was surprised by how much easier it was for Lisa to learn and play music pieces by heart and with assurance. Louise (who was in her 50s) was much more tentative in her playing and didn't even attempt to memorize the piano pieces.

Lisa then decided she really wanted to play the violin. I was amazed at how quickly she learned to read music and play the violin with assurance. Both girls took music lessons, but neither was really interested in pursuing a musical career. Neither practiced a lot. Lisa only practiced if she had a recital or performance coming up.

Most of this happened during the five years we lived in Oshkosh. Lisa's violin teacher led the orchestra in the high school in Oshkosh that Lisa was scheduled to attend before we decided to move to California. So, she was disappointed to lose a student with real potential. We were also disappointed to learn that California public schools had discontinued orchestra and music classes. We arranged for private music lessons for Lisa after we moved to San Diego County, but she did not persevere. Without the need to prepare for performances, she lost her motivation to continue.

Although opposite personalities, both girls were very strong persons. After those initial post-adoption months, I never had trouble relating to Ann. It was not that she never got angry with me anymore. Learning to drive was a good example. She took driving lessons at school in cars with automatic transmissions. We had a stick-shift Volkswagen, so I had to teach her how to drive with the stick shift. She learned quite well, but not without angrily complaining over and over. She just didn't understand why we couldn't have a car with an automatic transmission. Anyway, with Ann we learned to put up with her moods and were also amazed at how charming and cooperative she could be.

Lisa amazed us with her enthusiasm and eagerness to do things. She was always very curious and creative, but she used to make me really angry at times. It took me a while to realize it was her attitude toward authority that bothered me. I was the authority and she couldn't care less. She responded to competence, but not to someone's position and that was my hot button. Lisa would say things in a way that, in my experience, children did not say to parents or other adults.

ANN'S HIGH SCHOOL DAYS

Ann did well in high school in Oshkosh until her senior year when her grades slipped. She had met her first boyfriend. He was the brother of one of her classmates and had been in the military. Of course, this was a major distraction. We met Ann's boyfriend, but we never really got to know him.

We were concerned about her drop in grades; yet we were pleased that she was relating well with her classmates and with boys. Since she had not come on the American scene until she was 11, it was good that she was now able to enjoy a social life appropriate for her age group. She was not retreating into her introversion. So, we never made the drop in her grades an issue.

Ann came home from school one day and wanted to know what kind of parents we were. Taken aback we asked, "What do you mean?"

"Well," she said, "I'm the only kid in the whole high school who has never been grounded." Was she complaining? We laughed and told her we didn't think she had ever done anything that deserved grounding.

We were interested in what was happening with her friend and classmate relationships, but we tried not to pry. Louise pointed out to me that, if we waited, Ann would eventually tell us about how her social life was going.

I'm sure Ann didn't tell us everything. I'm also sure she probably did some things we wouldn't have approved of, or would have found upsetting. For example, years later she told me that she'd been in a speeding contest in our car with some of her high school friends. I was just grateful to know that no one was hurt. Basically, it came down to trust. We trusted Ann and she never gave us a reason not to trust her.

In 1988, the summer before Ann's senior year in high school, we took a two-week vacation trip out West. Ann objected to going on this trip. She wanted to stay behind and spend time with her boyfriend and class-mates. She even mentioned the possibility of having a party while we were gone. That was the last thing we wanted, having heard of the problems that occurred at such unchaperoned teen parties in the past. Ann did come with us on the trip, but reluctantly.

We first drove through Minnesota where Lisa got to visit the house written about in a book she loved: *Little House on the Prairie* by Laura Wilder.

We were awed by the Devil's Tower in North Dakota. We drove for miles looking for buffalo in a South Dakota park, but didn't see any. We were disappointed and left the park when it was getting dark. Then, a short distance down the highway, our car ran into a large herd of buffalo crossing the road and milling all around our car. It was a fantastic experience, but also more than a bit scary!

We visited Mount Rushmore and the caves of the cliff dwellers in Colorado. Then we went on to Yellowstone National Park where we woke up to see buffalo just outside the window of our cabin. We had to be concerned about the air quality because that was the year Yellowstone was on fire. I had never visited the American West and was simply enthralled by it all.

Al, Ann & Lisa on Family Trip Out West, 1988

Ann really enjoyed the trip, but never let on that she did at the time. Recently she talked about wanting to go back to Yellowstone. She reminisced about what a great time she had there, and wanted her husband Jim and her daughter Sara to experience it as well.

FAMILY TRIP TO SOUTH KOREA

Prior to our moving to Southern California in Summer 1989, the four of us flew to South Korea so that the girls could visit with their biological extended family, Louise could have direct experience of the Korean people and their culture, and I could observe how much South Korea had changed since I left the country in 1970.

Ann and Lisa's paternal grandparents, aunts, uncles, and cousins greeted us on our arrival at the Seoul airport. Their grandmother was very disappointed that Ann could not (or would not) converse with her in Korean. But Ann seemed to understand most of what was being said.

We enjoyed visiting temples and other cultural sites in and around Seoul with the family, and also took a bus trip to Sorak San in the mountainous area near the DMZ (the Korean Demilitarized Zone) at the border with North Korea. At one point, soldiers stopped our bus and checked for anything suspicious. When we climbed one of the nearby mountains, Louise was amazed to see Korean women dressed in nice suits, dresses and shoes rather than casual attire, climbing along with us.

The highlight of our visit to South Korea was renting a van and driving down to the family property in the rural village where the girls had lived before coming to America. No one was living in the family compound at the time—they were all living in Seoul. As we drove through the gate and saw the typical Korean farmhouse ahead of us, Ann remarked, "What a dump. Don't leave me here!"

Lisa, on the other hand, loved being back in the countryside she had enjoyed exploring freely as a child too young to go to school (whereas Ann, being older, had had to mind her sister and help with the chores, besides going to school!). Lisa would have liked to stay there longer. Ann enjoyed showing us her school and the long distance she had to walk back and forth between the family farmhouse and the school.

While we were there the family cooked a meal in the kitchen of the traditional Korean farmhouse with the ondol floor that I described in Chapter Three. Because it was a warm summer day, we felt the heat coming from the kitchen as we sat on the ondol floor eating a traditional Korean meal.

The family also led us to a plateau atop a hill near the farmhouse which turned out to be the family burying ground. While we were there, the family conducted a Confucian-type ceremony honoring their ancestors. Louise and I believed that this was also their way of recognizing us as Ann and Lisa's parents and we found this very touching.

*Lisa, Ann & Al with Aunt, Uncles & Cousins
Sightseeing in Seoul, Korea, 1989*

This visit to South Korea was the last time the girls would see their Korean grandparents. They passed away not long after our visit. Ann visited South Korea with her daughter Sara a few years ago and met some of her biological family members then. To this day she remains in contact with the Korean uncle who will later be described as not appreciating Lisa's "lip" while she stayed with him and his family briefly when she was a teenager.

LISA'S HIGH SCHOOL DAYS

Lisa's high school experience was quite different from Ann's. As previously mentioned, I expected that Lisa would display some acting out behavior in her teen years. The emotional load she carried from losing her birth parents and family and being sent off to America was bound to catch up with her. Lisa was most likely experiencing an identity problem and didn't feel sure that she really belonged here in America.

Before the adoption, I remember wondering how I would feel about having Korean children in our predominantly Caucasian society. After the adoption, this never occurred to me. I never thought of Ann and Lisa as foreigners or as strange or different in any way. To Louise and me, they were just our girls. However, their being Asian in a predominantly white social milieu did affect them to some extent. I remember Lisa as a young child looking at her beautiful black hair, wondering if it might turn blonde like Louise's.

The summer after Ann graduated from high school and Lisa was due to start high school, we moved from Oshkosh, Wisconsin to Carmel Valley, a community adjacent to Delmar in San Diego County, California. Louise had taken a teaching position in the School of Nursing at the University of San Diego (USD).

Lisa attended the nearby Torrey Pines High School as a freshman. The school had a very good academic reputation and we thought Lisa would do well there; however, she found it very difficult to make friends. Many students attending this high school were from families in higher socioeconomic brackets, as evidenced by the expensive luxury cars many of them were driving. There were also cliques already formed by students at their previous schools.

Lisa started out not knowing anyone and wasn't able to make friends easily. She told about trying to be friendly, making an effort to say hello to class-mates who then would simply turn and walk away. Lisa never felt at home at Torrey Pines High School; however, she did well academically and completed her freshman year without much complaint.

We moved to Encinitas, California the following year and suggested that Lisa change schools to San Dieguito High School which was located in Encinitas. San Dieguito High School also had a good academic rep-utation, but there were fewer students from wealthy families attending. Lisa started off well and made some good friends among other Asian students. However, her grades slipped in her junior year and she became rather depressed. She mentioned two problems: her Asian friends had all dropped out of high school so she didn't have anyone to eat lunch with, and she was hav-ing trouble concentrating on her studies.

Lisa was obviously very intelligent so I found it dif-ficult to take her academic complaints very seriously. However, she was unhappy and wanted to drop out of high school like her friends had. We consented to this but supported her attending evening school where she finished the work necessary to get her General Educational Development (GED) diploma.

We also arranged to have Lisa see a psychiatrist who had a reputation for working well with Asians. This helped somewhat, but she was still basically unhappy. She wrote some poems that were rather on the dark side. She was struggling with her identity. We were concerned, but not sure what to do.

Now that she wasn't going to school, Lisa started working as a waitress in a local sushi restaurant. One day she announced that she wanted to go back to South Korea. She called her uncle in Seoul and asked if she could live with him for six months. He agreed. Lisa had saved her money and had enough to pay for her airfare and to give something to her uncle for her room and board. When Lisa landed in Seoul she moved in with her uncle's family, which included his wife, two sons, and a daughter close to her age.

We thought that her exposure to the Korean culture and language would be good for her. While there, Lisa met her birth mother, who she reported was happy to see her. But Lisa told us later that she had felt nothing toward her birth mother. The most astounding outcome of their meeting was Lisa finding out that she had a full sister who didn't know that either she or Ann existed. Evidently our daughters' Korean birth mother had been pregnant with this child when she deserted their father's family after his death. And her birth mother indicated that she had no intention of ever telling this younger daughter about Ann and Lisa.

Unfortunately, Lisa's getting along with her Korean uncle was problematic. True to form, she had many arguments with her uncle. This was very un-Korean. In South Korea the father of the family was the authority figure and was accustomed to being treated with respect at all times. And here was a brash American teenager not afraid to argue with him. One of her arguments was about her cousins. The boys were given special treatment and there were plans for them to go to college. Their sister also wanted to go to college, but her father wasn't concerned about her wish to do so. Lisa didn't think that was fair and told her uncle so.

In any case, after being in South Korea for only four months , Lisa called and told us she was coming home early. She had decided she wanted to get ahead with her life in America. She was going to come home and attend college. I think her uncle was glad to see her go. He told Lisa it would be best that she not revisit South Korea for at least five years. She told him she would not return for at least ten years. I wrote that Lisa stayed in South Korea for four months. Lisa has insisted that it was only two months. Of course, I still thought that I was correct. Oh, and it's many more years later and Lisa has still never returned to South Korea.

ANN'S COLLEGE EXPERIENCES

Having finished high school in Oshkosh, Ann intended to go to college. Since her high school grades had slipped, she didn't qualify for admission to the University of San Diego. This hurt because she could have enjoyed free tuition all four years at this expensive private university because Louise was on the faculty. Instead, Ann attended community college for a year and then transferred to the California State University at Northridge.

When we drove her up to the Cal State Northridge campus, Ann found that the dorm room to which she had been assigned was very bare, her desk was broken, and the room was uncomfortably hot. Her roommate, whom she didn't know, wasn't there yet. It was a depressing introduction to this new phase of her life, so it was hard to leave her there.

That same evening we got a phone call from Ann. She was crying and said she hated it there. I told her that, if she found it too unbearable, she should come home.

Ann responded, "No." Once she put her mind to something, Ann persevered. Since she had her own car, she was able to drive home every weekend. She ultimately managed to adjust to college life and did well academically.

Not being sure what her major should be, she chose to major in history by default. Then, toward the end of her freshman year at Cal State Northridge, Ann remarked to us that a friend of hers was transferring to the University of Nevada Las Vegas (UNLV) to study hotel management.

Louise lit up. It sounded to her like something Ann would like and be good at, because she was so practical-minded and a natural organizer. Ann had worked for several years as a waitress in different restaurants and quickly figured out how each place could be reorganized for better customer satisfaction. You could tell she would have been comfortable running a restaurant. She didn't get into any conflict with her bosses and certainly wasn't telling them what they could do better. But her practical mind and organizational skills enabled her to know what would make for a smoother-running restaurant.

So, off we went to visit UNLV where Ann was interviewed and accepted into the School of Hotel Management. Incidentally, the semester after Ann left Cal State Northridge, the Northridge area experienced a strong earthquake that damaged several campus buildings. She had left the school at an opportune time!

Ann rented an apartment in the part of Henderson, Nevada known as Green Valley and found a job as a hostess at a nearby restaurant. This helped pay for her school and apartment expenses. It was while working there that she met Jim Petty, a frequent patron of the restaurant. At the time he was involved with another woman, but that relationship was ending. Ann was attracted to him. By Christmas she was deeply in love and hoped that her relationship with Jim would evolve.

We met Jim briefly in December 1993. He seemed to be a very nice man, but was 19 years older than Ann. In Spring 1994 he proposed and then Ann told us more about him. Besides being older, he was divorced and had 13-year-old twin sons and an 11-year-old daughter who were living with their mother.

I asked Ann if she knew what she was getting into. She insisted she did and could handle it. I told her the chances were very good that she would eventually have to help raise those children. She responded that she was prepared to do so.

I said, "No matter what, you have to finish your schooling and get your degree. Never knowing what the future holds, you need something to fall back on."

She agreed and with Jim's support received her Bachelor's Degree in Hotel Management from UNLV in 1995.

LISA'S COLLEGE EXPERIENCES

When Lisa came home from Korea, she signed up at the local community college for a full class load. Halfway through the semester she dropped most of her classes—surprisingly, all but calculus. She said she liked her calculus professor. He evidently made the classes interesting.

Lisa complained that she couldn't concentrate. I was thinking, *Come on, you can concentrate in calculus class but not in the easier classes?* Then Lisa got notice that she was on probation for not carrying enough classes. It surprised her to learn that she was in danger of being kicked out.

That summer, Louise attended a nursing conference in Colorado and took Lisa with her. On their return they had a long delay in the Denver airport. To pass the time, Louise read the latest issue of *Time* magazine with a cover story about young people with attention deficit disorder (ADD). The article described girls with ADD who didn't manifest the usual hyperactivity symptoms. Louise couldn't believe how accurately the description fit Lisa.

Louise showed the article to me when she returned home. We decided to have Lisa tested by a psychologist, who determined that she had mild ADD and recommended that she try Ritalin. We left it up to Lisa to take the drug and decide if and when she needed to take it. She found out that it did help her to concentrate. So, she took it before certain classes, and especially at test times.

After that she no longer had any trouble with her classes and eventually raised her grade-point average enough to qualify for admission to the University of San Diego where Louise was teaching. Lisa earned a bachelors degree in education and graduated with honors in 1999.

At the time of Lisa's ADD diagnosis, I was figuratively kicking myself. I had graduate-level credentials in school psychology and had tested many children for learning disabilities. Yet I had failed to see that Lisa had any learning problem. I was misled by her intelligence and lack of hyperactivity and violated my own rule, which was to always believe children when they told me they had a problem. Children don't tell you that as an excuse to avoid something they don't like. They usually really do have a problem and it had been my job to find out exactly what Lisa's was. I had let Lisa down. I was so grateful that Louise had been sharp enough to pick up on it.

The psychologist had noted how disinterested Lisa was during the testing he administered. She made no effort to please him or to try to excel. She was true to her nature; she just didn't respond to authority figures that way.

Lisa showed this same kind of attitude later, when she was a student at USD. As part of USD's core curriculum, Lisa was required to take one or two religion classes. At our urging, she signed up to take one of Dr. Bernard Cook's classes. He was a nationally known sacramental theologian, who Louise and I knew personally to be an exceptional person. She took the class, but never hesitated to remind Dr. Cook that she was an atheist. He had no trouble with this and Lisa took his class seriously.

ANN'S MARRIAGE

Ann convinced us of the rightness of her relationship with Jim, despite the fact that he was 19 years older and divorced. She told Louise and I that she had dated many guys, but after about five minutes always found they had nothing more to talk about. To the contrary, she found Jim very easy to converse with.

The ability to communicate is so important in marriage and Ann was not always the easiest person with whom to communicate. If she didn't feel like talking, she didn't, no matter what the situation. So, her finding Jim easy to communicate with was very convincing to us.

Ann and Jim arranged to meet us in San Diego in Spring 1994 so Jim could ask for our approval of their marriage. He told us later about how nervous he was. As the head of Air Vegas, a small airline established by his father to fly tourists from Las Vegas to the Grand Canyon, Jim never had trouble talking to senators (e.g., Senator John McCain, for one) and bigwigs in the airline industry. But that day he was nervous. Our reply to his asking for our blessing on their marriage was that we trusted Ann and we would stick by her judgment. Jim joyfully popped open the champagne!

Ann and Jim married in August 1994 and honeymooned in the Mediterranean. On their return, Ann called me crying. Jim's ex-wife had decided to move to Northern California for six months and Jim would have to take care of his three children during that time. I told Ann that I had warned her something like this might happen.

"Yes," she said, but she hadn't expected it to happen so soon. This meant that she and Jim would lose their privacy so soon after their wedding.

Once Ann set her mind on getting something accomplished, however, she persevered and always exceeded expectations. The three children moved in and Ann took on the role of mother: attending athletic and school events, food shopping, and cooking family meals, etc. Even though Ann had told Jim she didn't cook, she set about the task and quickly learned how.

At home, Jim and Ann played games with the children and saw to their schooling. This went on for four months. Then Jim's ex-wife returned and the children went back to live with her. Louise and I suspected that she returned sooner than expected because she learned about what a good job at mothering Ann was doing—again exceeding expectations!

How did Ann learn to cook? She started with a cookbook I gave her that had very detailed pictures for every step. I had gotten that cookbook because I planned to learn how to cook myself. The book wasn't detailed enough for me, though, so I never used it. For one thing, the cooking terminology was "Greek" to me. As with learning Latin and then Korean, it turned out that I was also a slow learner when it came to the culinary arts.

Incidentally, Ann knew how to prepare one dish well before she married—pasta primavera made with a white cream sauce. It was always my favorite. When she telephoned to say that she was fixing pasta primavera for dinner and asked "Would you like to come over?" I never refused the invitation. Whenever I ordered pasta primavera in a restaurant, however, it always came with a red sauce and I was always disappointed.

Today, Jim's daughter, Emi, is married and lives in Texas. She finished college in three years, earned a Master's Degree and now runs her own business in the field of occupational therapy. She's both an accomplished young woman careerwise and the mother of two very smart and active boys.

Jim's sons have very responsible jobs in the computer field. Jess moved to Los Angeles, married Melissa in May 2017, and now has a daughter and a son. Ely has lived in the Las Vegas area since high school and married in 2023. Both sons and their significant others are always welcome at Jim and Ann's house.

Ann and Jim tried hard to have a child of their own, but were unsuccessful. So, they decided to adopt and became the proud parents of a baby girl in September 1997. They named her Sara Louise.

Sara has always been an avid reader and did very well in elementary and high school. In 2018 she earned a bachelor's degree in music performance at Chapman University in Orange, California. Sara loves music and is especially skilled at playing the oboe and the English horn. She is as tall as Louise and is beautiful, poised, and outgoing—simply delightful to be with.

I especially enjoyed the fact that Sara loved to play cards, too, and would play with us whenever the opportunity presented itself. Ann, however, doesn't enjoy cards and only plays with us occasionally and reluctantly. Lisa never plays!

During her senior year at Chapman University Sara met Gabriel Martin, a jazz trumpet player. They started dating and became engaged a year or so later. Sara earned a masters degree in music performance at the University of Southern California in 2021 and immediately enrolled in a doctoral program there with the goal of teaching music to children, as well as performing. Louise was happily surprised to learn that it was her having earned a doctoral degree that strongly influenced her granddaughter to pursue one as well.

LISA'S MARRIAGE

In 1998, Lisa married Tony, a young man from a Catholic family of Italian descent who had graduated from San Diego State University. Tony, as well as Lisa, no longer attended church, much to his mother's dismay. So, Lisa and Tony were married on the grounds of our condominium complex in Encinitas, California by Joe Buko (Bukovchik), another former Maryknoll priest who had continued to function as a priest, especially by officiating at marriages.

Lisa's and Tony's son, Andrew, was born in March 2000 and they attended a Roman Catholic church long enough to have him baptized. To Lisa's surprise, she enjoyed the Mass liturgy. Although she didn't continue attending Mass, Lisa claims that she is no longer an atheist. She and Tony both went on to get their Master's degrees in business-related fields and have responsible, demanding jobs.

Lisa and Tony had some good years together. We always enjoyed their visits. Tony was an avid card player, so we could always count on some great canasta games with Tony during their visits. Tony, the "jock", liked to trash talk when he won, claiming he had "sent me to the woodshed". That kept me laughing. He also loved to tell me that the lightly-sweetened dark chocolate I loved tasted to him like "tree bark."

As mentioned before, Lisa never enjoyed playing cards or games. Andrew, on the other hand, took after his father and joined in the games as soon as he was old enough. But Andrew's real passion growing up was playing computer games. He would wait until everyone retired. Then he would contact a distant friend and they would compete playing computer games half the night.

Unfortunately, after 15 years of marriage, Lisa divorced Tony in 2013. Emotionally they had grown apart, but they continued to cooperate fully in ensuring that Andrew's needs were met. Lisa and Tony shared custody of Andrew and he spent alternate weeks with them through high school. Tony is a good father and has continued to support Andrew and do a lot of things with and for him through the years.

After high school, Andrew started college courses at the University of Utah. After taking an Introduction to Engineering course, which he found very boring, he decided to major in mathematics instead of engineering—aiming to become a high school math teacher. To Louise and my surprise and delight, Andrew transferred to Nevada State College in Henderson (where we lived) to pursue this major and lived with us during the Fall 2021 semester. It was a great opportunity to get to know our grandson better.

Andrew also worked at the Coca-Cola store on the Las Vegas Strip and learned how to make different Coke-based drinks that had been concocted in countries around the world. For Christmas he gave me a huge Coca-Cola jigsaw puzzle that took Louise and I forever to complete. We vowed never to try putting that puzzle together again!

In January 2022 Andrew decided to move back to San Diego because the Nevada State program did not turn out to meet his expectations. He reclaimed his job at a local Staples store in San Diego and has begun taking some online Purdue University business courses. Lisa, his mom, just wants him to ultimately earn a degree in something!

A year or so after her divorce, Lisa joined two strangers for a round of golf at a local San Diego golf course. These brothers didn't expect much by way of golf expertise from this petite Asian woman, but she surprised them. Loren, one of the two guys, is now married to Lisa and they live together in San Diego. He is also a dog lover and between them they have four dogs—two pugs and two mutts. When they came for a visit, sometimes the dogs came, too. As long as we didn't have to walk or feed them, that was just fine.

One of Lisa's passions has been growing things. We once thought she would study horticulture or landscape design in college. Despite not having a large yard, she has many fruit and vegetable-bearing trees and plants. When Lisa visits us she always brings shopping bags full of whatever is in season, including fruit (oranges, lemons, limes, tangerines, apples, persimmons, and/or bananas) and vegetables (avocados, tomatoes, peppers and/or zucchini) from her garden.

Al and Louise, daughters, husbands, and grandchildren in 2003

It has been a joy to watch our grandchildren grow up, just as it has been a wonder to watch Ann and Lisa mature in so many wonderful ways.

CHAPTER 7

My Awakening to Communication with the Spirit World

MANY PEOPLE ARE SKEPTICAL WHEN CONFRONTED WITH claims made by psychics, mediums, and intuitives that they can communicate with the spirits of those who have passed on. I, myself, was a skeptic for many years. I considered myself to be an intelligent, rational person who was not going to be fooled by impossible stories that can't be proven.

Then, in the mid-1990s, I read Rosemary Altea's book, *The Eagle and the Rose*. It was the first book that made me question my skeptical attitude. I believed in God, in angels, and in saints who intercede for the living, as well as in a continuation of life on a spiritual plane after death. However, I questioned whether some people had special psychic gifts and could communicate with the spirits of the dead. Altea's description of her childhood and her gradual realization that she had psychic gifts seemed to ring true. She didn't appear to be lying or trying to fool anyone. She was simply telling her story.

Then I read many other books by psychics, mediums, or intuitives, such as: John Edward, Sylvia Browne, John Holland, and James Van Praagh, as well as William James' studies of the paranormal and Raymond Moody's investigations of near-death experiences. Gary E. Schwartz at the University of Arizona has done research on the performance of mediums in controlled laboratory settings. I also found the work of Carlos Castaneda and Alberto Villoldo regarding shamanism to be especially interesting.

For the skeptic there is no absolute, indisputable scientific evidence of psychic gifts. It seemed to me that the claims of psychics can neither be proven or disproven scientifically. Neither can the existence of God or any purely spiritual reality be proven scientifically, yet millions of people believe in the existence of God and the existence of the spirit world. They do so based on their personal experience.

As I mentioned before, my wife, Louise, was a nurse with a doctoral degree in nursing education from Teachers' College, Columbia University. For many years, she taught undergraduate and graduate nursing students and was always interested in complementary therapies and holistic approaches to health care.

So, in 2000 both of us attended a Holistic Nursing Conference on Therapeutic Touch at Pacific Grove, California. Most of those attending the conference were nurses and I stood out as the only male and non-nurse attendee. I was simply accompanying

Louise, satisfying my curiosity and wanting to watch the energy healers who were there to practice therapeutic touch.

On the last day of the conference, Louise and I spoke with a young nurse who told us she practiced Reiki, saw auras, and knew her spirit guides. Spirit guides are described as spiritual entities that help and protect a living human being and communicate with that person through intuition, dreams, coincidences, or other signs. Some are people who have died and are now spirits living on the other side who may have a connection with an individual before or after that person's birth.

So, a spirit guide may be someone a person knew, either from this life or from a previous life, who watches over this individual and is willing to help if their assistance is requested. They never tell a person what to do. A person may or may not become aware of their guide's suggestions, since they often take subtle, non-verbal forms.

This young nurse told us that her spirit guide was currently very upset with her because she was not paying attention. I told her I didn't know if I had a spirit guide and, if so, it was the guide's fault if I didn't listen because the guide had never made his/her presence known to me. I had always believed in guardian angels, but had never felt their presence either.

Later that afternoon Louise and I boarded a small commuter plane for our return flight to San Diego. I was seated in the front row with Louise sitting to my right next to the window. The aisle was to my left.

I thought Louise was trying to get my attention and said aloud, "Louise?" Then I saw that she was reading and wasn't even aware of me at that moment. I looked around. The aisle was empty and everything seemed normal. I shrugged, wondering what had happened, then decided to go back to sleep.

I was just drifting off when I suddenly felt a touch on my left cheek. My eyes were closed when I mentally saw a white, foggy-looking face with indistinct features right up against my face. The visage disappeared as suddenly as it had appeared. I opened my eyes and found that nothing around me had changed. Everything was just as it had been.

I knew this visage had been in my face on the left side away from Louise on purpose, so I would not think it was Louise. I knew it was not something my imagination had conjured up. This phenomenon was entirely outside of me.

I had flippantly denied that I had any spirit guide and that, if I did, it was up to the spirit guide to make him/herself known to me. So, all I could conclude was that he/she had just done that. I intuited that this guide was a woman and knew it was not a dream. I thanked my guide for showing herself to me and felt rather awestruck.

I never had any repeat of this kind of experience. However, I did have two significant vivid dreams, spaced out with years between them, in which a woman made her presence known. These dreams were different from the face-to-face encounter described above, except that I knew the woman was real and outside of me. It was not my imagination. I couldn't say whether it was the same woman in the vivid dreams on all three occasions. But I felt that the woman in each dream was someone I knew, even though I saw nothing that clearly identified her.

These experiences convinced me that genuine psychics, intuitives, and mediums describe psychic experiences that are real. More and more people seem to be acknowledging such events in their own lives and are beginning to value their own psychic gifts, rather than fearing and repressing them.

From what I read about them, most true psychics/intuitives/mediums say that they are not really so different from other people because everyone has some degree of innate psychic ability that can be developed. That is also true of athletic ability, but there are very few athletes who can develop their potential to become as good as, for example, Babe Ruth, Serena Williams, Michael Jordan, Simone Biles, or Tom Brady.

MY REAL-LIFE ENCOUNTERS
WITH AN INTUITIVE/MEDIUM

Although I had done a lot of reading about intuitives and mediums, I never really expected to meet one. Knowing how much the well-known mediums charge for their services, I knew they were way out of my financial league. Prior to meeting Suzanne (as described in the next section), the closest I ever came to meeting one was attending several conference sessions presented by famous mediums like James Van Praagh and John Edwards and observing the amazing connections between audience members and their deceased loved ones that occurred through their mediumship.

Then, one winter evening in 2005 Louise and I attended a singing bowl meditation at Stillpoint, a local Las Vegas center devoted to promoting spiritual development. We were there mainly because we were curious about this type of meditation.

During singing bowl meditations, seven crystal or brass bowls of different sizes are struck continuously and their respective resonances match those of our seven chakras or energy centers. The leader plays the bowls for about 50 minutes while the participants sit or lie in comfortable positions and let the sounds reverberate around and through them. Louise and I both found this type of meditation extremely relaxing.

Suzanne, the woman who played the bowls, introduced herself beforehand as a Native American. She told us that she had the following gifts: she was clairaudient, clairvoyant, clairsentient, and clairkinetic. She stated that she could see and influence the color changes in the auras (or energy fields) surrounding our bodies as she played the bowls. Suzanne claimed she was an intuitive and a medium, but not a psychic. She made this distinction because she said psychics predict the future (which she does not do).

When the meditation was over, we hung around to talk with Suzanne. She looked at me and told me I had a "blood sucker" hanging onto me. I was amused, thinking she was joking. Suzanne insisted and I laughingly denied knowledge of any such thing. All this time she was busy packing up the bowls and preparing to leave. I asked her about her psychic gifts, especially if she found them hard to accept. She responded she had to go, but we could talk later if I wanted to do so.

After I arrived home, it hit me. I realized that a distant acquaintance could be described as the "bloodsucker" who had tried to draw energy from me. This individual had repeatedly sought my attention by contacting me at odd, unpredictable, inconvenient times. I knew that this person had experienced many troubles, and found it easier to talk with me than to deal realistically with these problems. Both as a married priest and as a counselor I had felt I should listen because something I would say might be of help.

Later in the week I called Suzanne and asked if we could meet. She arranged to meet Louise and me in a local Starbucks one afternoon. The weather was unusual for the Las Vegas area that day—it had rained almost continually. We met Suzanne at the Starbucks between 2 and 3 p.m. and talked for more than two hours. I had forgotten most of the details, but remembered that she talked about auras, told us things communicated to her about Louise's father (who died when Louise was 14), and said she was aware of the presence of spirits in the Starbuck's that Louise and I could not perceive.

Of course, we could not prove that anything Suzanne said was true, but she told us some things about our lives that convinced us she was speaking the truth, that her gifts were real. This made us want to learn more. We offered to take Suzanne to dinner that evening and we met with her and her husband and daughter in a busy, local Mexican restaurant where the food was excellent.

During the dinner conversation we learned that Craig, her husband, was an artist who specialized in pottery throwing and that her son was currently in the army and stationed in Iraq. Craig invited us to participate the following weekend in a long day of firing pottery according to the Japanese raku method. I had never heard of the raku method, so this was all new to me. After our pottery bowls were formed and painted, they were fired in a large can of burning trash to glaze the coating. The small bowls we made were neat and decorative, but could not be used as food containers.

FURTHER ENCOUNTERS WITH SUZANNE

Suzanne had a storefront business called "A Heartline Center" where she practiced massage and other holistic therapies and conducted intuitive readings. She worked with two other massage therapists, one of whom specialized in treating horses. Suzanne also practiced as a midwife in a nearby native American reservation and was transported as needed to and from the reservation via helicopter.

As a medical intuitive, Suzanne could identify physical health problems when she laid hands on a person. If the health problem was a potentially serious one, she recommended that the person consult a medical doctor. This scared many people and, since denial was a common response, Suzanne became selective about whether to tell a person what she had discovered concerning their health through her laying on of hands.

Louise and I both scheduled an appointment with her. Louise went first and received a massage and a body reading. During my appointment I told Suzanne I was more interested in having a reading wherein she communicated with spirits from the other side than in receiving a massage. We agreed to split the hour, using the first half-hour for a reading and the second half-hour for a massage. The reading lasted 50 minutes. Since only ten minutes were left, Suzanne did a quick relaxation massage. After that first appointment, I never received a full massage from Suzanne, only very short ones for specific physical problems.

My readings with Suzanne continued but became less frequent as time went on. The sessions usually began with me asking all sorts of questions. She never answered my questions with a simple "yes" or "no". There was always a long answer or explanation. The readings often left me feeling enlightened in some ways and confused in other ways.

Some people would have called me gullible. I didn't believe everything she said, especially when she talked about the future. When she did so, she always added that there are many factors influenced by free will that can change an eventuality. Therefore, she always insisted that she was an intuitive, not a psychic who predicted the future.

Based on my experience, I believed that Suzanne was a remarkable intuitive. The following paragraphs describe two encounters with her, among many, that surprised me and gave me confirmation as to her authenticity.

During my second or third reading, Suzanne asked if triangles had any special meaning for me. My answer was a firm "No." I questioned why she asked about triangles. Suzanne said she didn't know, but it had something to do with a visit. She then dropped the subject and went on to other matters. It was an odd question. Perhaps, I thought, in the future I could watch for something triangular, like a sculpture or a building or something else wherever I was visiting.

That reading was on a Monday or Tuesday. The following Friday, our daughter, Lisa, her husband, Tony, and our grandson, Andrew came up from San Diego for the weekend. On Saturday morning Louise and I took Andrew to a nearby park to watch our granddaughter, Sara, play soccer. It was a long walk from the parking lot to the playing field. I was walking in front; Louise and Andrew followed behind me. I was in a hurry to get to the playing field, but I stopped short when I heard Andrew say to Louise, "Look at all the triangles I have."

I turned to see five-year-old Andrew joining his hands so that his fingertips and thumbs touched to form multiple triangles. Suzanne could not have had foreknowledge of this particular situation. She had only been told by her angel guide that triangles and a visit were going to have some meaning for me. Andrew's forming the triangles with his fingers and telling Louise to look at them confirmed for me that

Suzanne really intuited that message about a visit and triangles from her angel guide.

The second encounter with Suzanne involved my sister-in-law, Mary Alice. Whenever Louise and I visited my family in Akron, Ohio we usually went out to dinner at least once with my brothers and sisters.

For a significant part of her life, Mary Alice had suffered from a very painful and deforming arthritis, but she always remained positive and rarely complained. Then she was diagnosed with cancer.

At the time of this particular dinner, we knew Mary Alice's cancer was terminal and that this was probably the last dinner we would share with her. Some people might find my question to Mary Alice to be insensitive, but I knew she was not afraid to talk about dying.

"Mary Alice" I asked, "if you die before I do, will you help me over when I pass?"

Mary Alice replied, "No."

Surprised, I asked her, "Why not?"

She answered, "I'm going to be too busy."

"Too busy? Doing what?" I asked.

"Praying for my grandchildren," she replied.

I laughingly agreed that this was a good reason.

This conversation with Mary Alice occurred before I met Suzanne and I never told her about it. During one of my readings, I asked Suzanne about certain relatives and friends who had passed. When I mentioned someone, Suzanne would tell me what they were doing on the other side. For example, she reported that my mother was resting, my father was gardening, and that they were present and wanted me to know they were well.

I asked if Mary Alice was present. Suzanne paused a minute and then said, "No, she's busy." About five minutes later, she quoted something a spirit was saying to her. When I asked who had said that, Suzanne told me it was Mary Alice.

I responded, "I thought she was too busy to be here."

Suzanne shrugged and said, "Well, she's here now."

I believed that Mary Alice was simply reminding me of our previous dinner conversation and used it to confirm that her spirit was really there.

One of the things I always found interesting about Suzanne was that, during the readings, she often repeated what the guides/spirits present were telling her to say. Most often she shared what the Archangel Raphael, her main spirit guide, was telling her. But there were always other spirits chiming in as well. She often quoted them like she was having an ordinary conversation, without looking up to the heavens or to any other place in the room. She didn't close her eyes or change her voice.

On occasion she would ask the unseen entity to: "Slow up. Say that again." Sometimes the spirits used words Suzanne didn't know or couldn't even pronounce correctly. At other times she would say, "One at a time. You're all talking at once."

During the readings Suzanne often asked me, "Do you understand that?" Because of the ordinary way she spoke, I often had to ask, "Are you saying that or is a spirit telling you what to say?" because it looked like Suzanne was having a casual conversation with an unseen someone.

LEARNING ABOUT MY SPIRIT GUIDES

Another interesting thing I learned from the many readings I had with Suzanne was the identity of my spirit guides. Over time, Suzanne identified five different spirit guides that hung around me. The most prevalent and verbal spirit she identified as Ben, the Maryknoll priest who was my good friend and seminary classmate. He had also been assigned to missionary work in South Korea after our ordination in 1959. Suzanne didn't know who my seminary classmates were, or that Ben was in charge of the orphanage where our adopted daughters, Ann and Lisa, stayed just before coming to the States. We visited him there in 1989 when we took our daughters back to Korea for a visit with their grandparents, uncles, aunts, and cousins.

Long after I had left Maryknoll, Ben volunteered to work as a priest on the Kamchatka Peninsula in far eastern Russia. I saw him for the last time at Maryknoll in 1999 at the 40th anniversary of our ordination and class reunion. Ben had been diagnosed with bone cancer and died in 2001.

During the early readings, Suzanne complained about Ben being a pest because he visited her at inopportune times. For example, she said he would visit during the night when she had forbidden any and all spirits to bother her. I laughed at this because it reminded me of Whoopie Goldberg's character in the movie *Ghost*.

A few years after I started having readings, Suzanne told me she didn't like former or married priests and that, initially, she wasn't interested in working with me. Ben insisted to her that I was different and that she needed to work with me. He was also concerned about the welfare of our daughters. At another time, Ben intervened to give Suzanne some advice that helped her deal with a problem in her own life. From then on, Ben was okay with her and continued to be a guide for both Suzanne and me.

Suzanne told me that my parents were often present during my readings, but usually just watched in the background. The only message from my mother that I remember Suzanne mentioning was when I had pneumonia in 2006. She related to me that my mother wanted me to know I wasn't going to die. I went for several days without sleep, but never felt I was in danger of dying from the pneumonia.

Another of my guides that Suzanne identified was Archangel Metatron. Metatron is an archangel said to contribute to spiritual understanding and to help one overcome procrastination, which was always a major problem for me. So, I felt that Metatron's help in this regard would be most welcome. When Suzanne first mentioned him, she didn't know much about him either, or even how to pronounce his name correctly. He was as new to her as to me.

I was skeptical about archangels as spirit guides for us lowly humans. I thought they were especially high-powered and above the human fray. Why would they show any interest in me? I later learned that angels enjoy being helpful to all of us, but only if we ask them. They offer help, but won't intervene unless we ask for their help. And, if you do not ask for or spurn their help, they have other things to do.

For years Suzanne mentioned a spirit guide named Abigail or Abby, whom I had never met in this life. Only later did I seek more information about her from Suzanne. The only reply I got was that Abigail loved me. I was amazed and really touched by this. At a later reading, I again asked what my connection with Abigail was and why she loved me. Suzanne then explained (speaking for Abigail, I assume) that in a previous life I was a stable boy who had been blamed for some sort of bad behavior. Although I was innocent, I had been beaten for it more than once. Abigail told Suzanne that she had cared for my wounds and comforted me.

Suzanne also identified another guide I found most interesting. For a long time, she spoke about a woman named Layla. Suzanne said she was someone I had known in this life. Layla is an unusual name; yet I couldn't remember meeting any woman named Layla.

During repeated readings, Layla's name kept coming up as a guide and someone I had known in this life. Suzanne said I knew her in Chicago and that there was something about a train ride and prayer. I had only been in Chicago a few times in my life and had no recollection of encountering any woman named Layla, riding in a train, or praying with her.

I was certain that Suzanne had this all wrong, but she insisted. I really wanted to know who this guide was, so I kept asking questions. Suzanne mentioned someone being a liaison, but she had trouble pronouncing the word "liaison" so that didn't help.

There was only one woman I could associate with Chicago, so I asked if this "Layla" had anything to do with "Ann from Japan."

Layla communicated "Yes" to Suzanne.

I asked if the train ride was in Japan. Again, the answer was in the affirmative. I had ridden the bullet train with Ann from Kyoto to Tokyo when I stopped in Japan on my way home from South Korea. She had been working in Japan at that time as an American volunteer. I had previously met with her briefly when she visited some of the Maryknoll missions in South Korea. She was one of the most dedicated, intelligent, and spiritual persons I'd ever met. I felt that she was a very special person.

While working in the pastoral counseling program at St. Luke's Hospital in New York City in 1970, I met Ann several more times. She was staying with girlfriends from South Korea or Japan, some of whom I knew. We always met in groups, usually to have dinner in a Manhattan restaurant. Ann and I talked about what we would do in the future, since we were both looking for work at the time. She eventually returned home to Madison, Wisconsin and then moved to Chicago to find work, whereas I found a job in New York City.

One winter day in 1971 I wanted to find out more about Ann, so I called and arranged to meet her in Chicago. She invited me to stay at her aunt's house where she was living temporarily. We had a great

weekend visiting an art museum, attending an eve-
ning performance by a famous singer (whose name
I couldn't remember), and viewing the movie *The
Boys in the Band*.

During the reading, Suzanne said that Layla was
Ann's aunt and that I had broken her blue teapot. I
vaguely remembered Ann's aunt, but not her name or
what she looked like. And I recalled clumsily bumping into the card table and knocking over and breaking her teapot. Although I was the one who knocked
it over, Ann's aunt apologized for the set-up and graciously assured me it was all her fault. I thought she
was a very unusual and kind woman.

As for Ann, I didn't really get to know her any
better during my Chicago visit. Despite all the time
we spent together, we never even held hands. I felt
very attracted to her, but never felt that the attraction was reciprocated. I left Chicago feeling that she
liked me and enjoyed my company, but that the relationship would never progress beyond that.

Ann wrote me later saying we could be friends.
By then I had met Louise, so I wrote to Ann and told
her I was seeing another woman. I knew that the
friendship was over. I was in love with Louise and
didn't want to be distracted by an attraction to
another woman. That Chicago visit was the last time
I saw Ann and our exchange of letters was the last
time I had any contact with her.

During the reading I asked Suzanne if Ann was
a lesbian. Suzanne answered affirmatively and said
that "lesbian" was the word she had mispronounced
as "liaison." I hadn't been sure about this, but had

often thought that her selection of *The Boys in the Band* movie for us to see together was an odd choice. Was it a hint about her sexual orientation?

Regardless, I learned a lot from that movie. Having been exposed to all the Catholic Church propaganda about the sinfulness of homosexuality, this was the first time I realized that homosexuality wasn't necessarily a question of sexual lust. The male characters in the film were truly in love with each other.

Finally, I asked Layla, through Suzanne, about Ann today. She communicated that Ann was still alive and had a partner. But she didn't tell me anything else about her life. I remembered Ann being one of the most extraordinary persons I had ever met and I was honored that her aunt was helping me as a guide.

More recently, Suzanne mentioned that a man who had been hanging around was another one of my guides. She told me she didn't know his name and that he stayed in the background and didn't talk. This man seemed to be present to Suzanne at lot during multiple readings over a period of several months, so I decided it was time to find out who he was.

All Suzanne could tell me was that he was a mentor who had helped me when I was leaving the priesthood. I had talked with several priests and non-Catholic ministers during that time, but I couldn't think of anyone I had consulted as a mentor. I kept wondering about this for several months, thinking this spirit guide must have been a priest or minister. It never occurred to me that he might have been a layman.

Then, one day it came to me. This spirit guide was the Jungian psychiatrist, Dr. Whitmont, whom I had seen for two or three years after I left Maryknoll. He had really helped me understand my feelings and adjust to life as a lay person. Suzanne's reference to that mysterious presence being a mentor then made sense, although I had never before thought of Dr. Whitmont in that way. I had had no contact with him in 40 years. So, it amazed me that he not only remembered me, but was also in some way helping to guide my life journey.

During one of the readings, Suzanne mentioned our daughter, Angela. I responded that we had no daughter named Angela. She insisted. I said our only daughter, other than Ann and Lisa, was the baby we aborted many years ago. We had named her Catherine Louise. I had never mentioned anything about the pregnancy or the abortion prior to this moment. Suzanne agreed that Angela was that child. She didn't say this, but I took her calling our baby Angela to mean that she was like an angel in heaven.

Suzanne then went on to say that our baby was okay with the abortion and that she had agreed to become our baby knowing the likelihood that the pregnancy would be terminated. I had forgotten the rest of the exact conversation, but it seemed like Catherine Louise was communicating to us that she didn't want us to feel guilty. She had agreed to the whole event for our learning and personal growth.

In fact, Louise and I hadn't felt guilty, just very sad because we had so much wanted to have Catherine Louise in our lives. This communication gave us an entirely different perspective on the abortion. We still grieved over our loss, but it was tremendously comforting to know that Catherine Louise had freely participated in the pregnancy and its termination out of love for us.

In another session some weeks later, Suzanne told me that Catherine Louise had been aborted again during another woman's pregnancy. And then, at an even later session, Suzanne said that Catherine Louise had been born successfully to a couple in the Northeast. When I asked if we might ever meet her there, Suzanne said, "No."

SUMMARY THOUGHTS AND INSIGHTS

I was immensely grateful for the new understandings of spirits and the spiritual world I gained from my readings with Suzanne. Those on the spirit plane are not limited to the space and time constraints that are so much a part of our lives in this world. We find it hard to think beyond these limits; yet, based on the understandings I gathered during my years having readings with Suzanne, human spirits who have passed on are no longer limited by space and time. For example, they can be in more than one place at a time, and time and space have no meaning for them. There is no space between them and us.

We tend to think of those who have passed away as being in a heavenly space somewhere up there separated from us. But spirits and the spirit world actually surround us. We "touch" them by our thoughts and they "hear" us if we address them. It seems to bother those who have died when we cannot accept losing them and continue to make ourselves unhappy over their departure.

The message seems to be for us to go on with our lives and know that our deceased loved ones are enjoying their spiritual existence and are ready to support us at all times. They would like to communicate with us, but most of us don't know how to hear or pay attention to their messages without the help of mediums/intuitives like Suzanne.

Because of my growing awareness of this spirit world that surrounds us, I came to believe that I was walking through heaven all the time, even though I was not always fully aware of it. Although the demands of daily life kept intruding and distracting me, I came to a deeper understanding of St. Catherine of Siena's famous saying, "The way to heaven is heaven, because He said 'I am the Way'."

I also came to believe that hell is a concept that needs to be rethought. I no longer considered hell to literally be a pit of fire where unrepentant, sinful souls suffer for all eternity. Instead, I came to understand that hell is best described as the absence of love and that we create our own hell (and punishment) whenever we refuse to love. Our main purpose on earth is to grow in our capacity to love God, our neighbor, and ourselves. People who refuse to love, who do not give or receive love, live in a hell of their own making.

The idea that we have only one chance in life and are stuck forever with who we are at the time of death and judgment no longer fit my understanding of God's creation. The belief that God is just waiting to judge and condemn us if we don't avoid evil in any form was always in the back of my mind for the first half of my life. This helped me to avoid evil, but I can't say it helped me form a positive image of God or the importance of love. The imaging of God as a loving Father came to mean more to me than any concept of a God who is a stern judge.

If life is eternal and God is infinite, why would He/She limit how much we can grow in love to one lifetime? I came to believe that reincarnation, returning to a new earthly life, is one option that can help a soul continue to grow. In this context, the movie *Groundhog Day* comes to mind, with its lesson that we have to keep coming back until we get it right. Or at least it's one of the options we have since we never lose free will. I came to believe that life in the spirit world (after we pass over) also involves a continued process of discovery and growth in love.

But what about truly evil people? For example, what happens to serial killers, evil dictators, child abusers, and the like after they die? Suzanne and her spirit guides were not completely clear about their fate. They assured me that evil people have no power to harm us when we reach the spiritual plane and, in some way, are segregated from those living in love. It is their hate and lack of love that segregates them. They maintain their free will so they can choose to learn to love. It must be a tremendously difficult choice for them to make, but they have all eternity to work at it.

I also asked Suzanne about people with whom I have been upset in this life, wondering if they realize their mistakes or the harm they have done. In particular, I asked whether Pope John Paul II, now that he is on the other side, realizes the harm he did as pope by suppressing all dialogue and dissent within the Roman Catholic Church? He did a lot of good in the world-at-large, but did he have any regrets about the repression he imposed within the Church? The answer always came back that there is no negativity in heaven, like it was none of my business. Instead, my job was to focus on practicing love and forgiveness in my own life here and now.

One of the most surprising things I learned during my readings with Suzanne was that people enter the spirit world with the same attitudes, convictions, family and social connections, and the same capacity to love others they had in this life. There doesn't seem to be a sudden enlightenment that causes a newly passed on spirit to change immediately. If they died with selfish prejudices, they take them with them. If they died with addictions, those too remain to be overcome. They can change; but, in some cases, this can only be done by reincarnating into another earthly lifetime. Some things can best be worked out on the earth plane.

We all know how difficult it can be to change someone's mind, to argue against prejudice, or to try to help someone overcome an addiction. Angels have the same problem trying to enlighten souls even on the spiritual plane. For example, my brother Paul died in 2014. When I asked Suzanne about Paul, she responded that, from the other side, he had asked her if she was a witch. Paul hardly ever expressed his opinions during his lifetime. But I felt he had had reservations about what Suzanne told me about Mary Alice, his deceased wife, in a previous reading. Although he had never met Suzanne, I think that his unspoken opinion about her, both before and after he died, was that she must be a witch.

Even though Paul was in the presence of angels and saintly beings, he did not understand who Suzanne was and the nature of her intuitive gifts. The departed have to start with who they were when they entered the spirit world and continue to strive to grow spiritually. Despite this, they are not suffering; that is, they are not in physical or emotional pain. Some may be unhappy with themselves, despite being lovingly accepted by all those around them, as they come to realize the negative aspects of the person they became (such as being prejudiced, selfish, or unforgiving).

When I asked about my brother Paul again later, Suzanne told me that he communicated to her that heaven was not what he thought it would be. At the time I didn't ask for clarification about what he meant. My impression was that he had been surprised that he wasn't suddenly enlightened and changed, and that he is realizing that life on the spiritual plane demands that one continue to work on overcoming negative, judgmental attitudes that block spiritual growth.

As mentioned in the beginning of this spiritual autobiography, I was truly just an ordinary guy who found it hard to forgive sometimes. In my judgment, Popes John Paul II, Benedict XVI, and many in the Roman Catholic Church hierarchy were not/are not very good at their jobs and have been too invested in protecting their power, authority, and privileges. Their stress on maintaining the party line and refusal to consider any ideas that differ from their own are distressingly sad. Talk about dictators! To me, they didn't seem to understand at all what the spiritual life is about. They are wrapped up in their rules and doctrines, considering them more important than the pastoral needs of the people. Whereas, Jesus taught that the rules are made for the people, not the people for the rules (Luke 6:2-22; Matthew 12:1-14).

The bureaucrats in the Roman Catholic Church hierarchy haven't seemed to realize that they have lost their credibility. How many bishops or cardinals would you choose to be your personal spiritual director? As an ordinary guy, what gave me the right to judge these "great" men? Was I any better? I hoped they were acting sincerely to fulfill what they perceived to be God's will, but I questioned that. Yet, as one who has often failed to live consistently according to the spirit of the Gospel, how could I condemn them? They could have called me a hypocrite too. Therefore, I had to forgive them, despite my deep disagreement with them.

I used to think how great it must be to have the intuitive gifts that Suzanne possessed. I thought intuitives/mediums had direct contact with the spiritual world and that this must make life a lot easier. I came to realize that their gifts are mainly for the good of others and actually make their own lives much more complicated. Suzanne has a full array of gifts that she can't ignore or get away from. They have always been complicating and interfering with her daily life. These gifts come with the responsibility to use them to help others. But they often really do make life more difficult for the intuitives, mediums, and psychics who are endowed with them.

CHAPTER 8

Becoming Open to Living
with Uncertainty

THE ROMAN CATHOLIC CHURCH HAS BEEN SUSPI-
CIOUS of mysticism and has tended to dismiss
or ignore it, not really accepting it as spiritually valid. Yes, the Church has recognized certain
saints who were mystics, such as St. Teresa of Avila
and St. John of the Cross. Even in their lifetimes,
however, they were considered suspect.

Most people are trying to live good lives in
accordance with their spiritual values. When they
read about or hear of the saints' mystical experiences, they think how wonderful they must be.
People who are striving to live spiritual lives wish
they could also enjoy those experiences.

For centuries writers about the spiritual life
have pointed out that mystical experiences are not
essential for spiritual growth. Absence of mystical
experiences does not mean that a person is not living a life of deep spirituality. I believed that the

essence of spirituality is one's love relationship with God and neighbor.

God is everywhere and in everything, so we are constantly in touch with God, immersed in God. The problem is that most of us aren't aware of the Divine Presence most of the time, as we go through our daily lives, because we don't feel it. We have to take this on faith. We long for a heightened awareness of the Divine Presence. We want God to reveal Him/Herself to us in some perceptible way. But we need to be able to recognize the subtle signs of the Divine Presence that are present in everything that happens to us in our everyday lives.

Often this isn't easy. For example, if another person is actively persecuting us, as happens in the abusive relationships so many people have to endure, where is God? If love and compassion are the measure of spirituality, the depth of our relationship with God, how can we love our enemies as Jesus taught? This doesn't mean that we have to accept abusive behavior. We have the right and duty to avoid and oppose it as much as we can. While we may hate the abusive behavior, Jesus taught us by word and example to forgive and have compassion for the abuser.

My main concern here has been that we generally tend to ignore or discourage visions or other intuitive experiences. Many people experience actual spiritual events but are afraid to talk about them, anticipating that they will be laughed at or that no one will believe them. For example, the visions of Mary at Medjugorje, Lourdes, and Fatima were viewed with doubt and suspicion for many years, but have since been approved by the Church.

There are, in fact, many people who can tell of visions or intuitive insights they have experienced. This doesn't necessarily mean they are crazy or that they are imagining it, or that it is merely wishful thinking. I believed this even though I have known persons whose experiences were definitely delusional.

Intuitive experiences are very normal/not unusual in the everyday life of individuals who have dared to open themselves up to their psychic/intuitive gifts. For instance, Theresa Caputo—the Long Island Medium—is an intuitive who communicates regularly with the spirits of the deceased. Some people may scoff at her mediumship, but those who have experienced her readings do not. They realize that Theresa has shared information concerning their deceased loves ones that she would have had no way of knowing. These communications have comforted them, relieved them of anxiety, and enabled them to accept their losses and achieve some level of peace.

In past centuries the Long Island Medium might have been institutionalized out of ignorance and fear, or even burned at the stake as a witch. Even today some would attribute her psychic abilities to the devil, claiming Satan is working through her. We cannot let fear allow us to avoid truth or to dismiss or make fun of psychic abilities or attribute them to evil.

Many intuitives/mediums/psychics live very spiritual lives, are fervent believers in God, and use their gifts/psychic abilities only to help other people. Their abilities have nothing to do with evil or devil worship or satanic power. They are normal human beings with special abilities and gifts that should be used for the benefit of others. It must be admitted that some individuals fraudulently present themselves as mediums and psychics; however, there are many mediums and psychics whose authenticity is confirmed by the truth of their communications. I came to believe that communication with the deceased by reputable mediums should be taken seriously.

Many people think of their deceased loved ones as being in a heaven that is a faraway place "up there" somewhere, ruled over by a God envisioned as an old man with a beard. However, God—the infinite spiritual Being who exists everywhere and sustains all creation — is our heaven. The souls or spirits of the deceased, like us, are all sustained in existence by God but, since they are pure spirits, time and place don't apply to them anymore.

When we pray or just think about deceased persons, I believed that we are instantly in communication with their spirits which are not far away—not "out there" somewhere. We are all surrounded by the spirits of the deceased. Unlike most of us, mediums are able to see, hear and/or feel their presence and communicate with them. The spirits of the deceased can also touch us spiritually by sending us signs or subtle messages. But we need to be attuned to recognizing them.

Mediums/intuitives often describe their gifts as abilities that they have developed over time. Everyone has the potential to develop these abilities to some degree, but most people have repressed them as a result of cultural conditioning. For example, being able to sing is generally considered a normal human ability, even though some people are tone deaf like I was and have no idea how other people sing in tune. Some individuals have developed their singing ability far beyond what the normal person can do. Accomplished vocalists don't consider it mystical or mysterious. Their singing ability has resulted from the development of a normal human capability.

The fact that one person can do something that the vast majority of people cannot do (for example, walk a tight rope) doesn't mean they're crazy. Some people have the rare ability to memorize a book simply by reading it once. It is an extraordinary and very rare gift, but it is a real human ability.

In like manner, mediums and psychics have special gifts and they're not crazy either. They aren't people to fear; instead, they should be appreciated for their courage in opening themselves up to being able to see, hear, or feel the presence of spirits. Individuals (especially children) who show signs of having intuitive/psychic abilities should be encouraged to develop them and taught to use them for the good of the rest of us.

Spirits are aware of and understand us if we mentally talk to or think about them, but most of us cannot hear them reply. They can also communicate with us nonverbally through subtle or not-so-subtle signs, such as a light going on and off, or a picture falling off a shelf, or the radio playing a meaningful song.

I experienced a "not so subtle" sign after Suzanne told me to watch for a bird (and not an ordinary bird like a pigeon) at my sister Roseanna's burial in Cleveland, Ohio. Since health problems prevented me from traveling there from Las Vegas, I alerted my niece to watch out for such a bird at the burial site.

My niece later reported that after the burial, but before she and other relatives left the site, they were startled when a red-tailed hawk suddenly swooped down right over their heads. Later, Suzanne confirmed that the hawk was my sister communicating that she was there. We tend to dismiss such signs as accidents or unexplainable coincidences, even though they may actually represent a spirit trying to communicate with us.

Truths can be communicated to us from the other side through the mouths of mediums, as well as through earthly truth-tellers. When we dismiss truths that don't fit in with our belief system, we cheat ourselves. It is important to be open and able to integrate truths from different sources. This may involve questioning our beliefs as objectively as possible and admitting that we, as humans, are not infallible and can be wrong. By questioning our beliefs, we can change and grow; otherwise, we are destined to die defending indefensible prejudices.

More important than our intellectual belief system is our faith, our personal relationship with God, our lived experience of the Divine Presence. There is a lot about the spiritual life that we don't understand as we search for meaning and purpose, and try to live by the values that guide our lives. Truth, as

God's revelation, brings us to an awareness of God. And, because God is all about unconditional love, the spiritual life is more a matter of the heart than of the mind.

The Roman Catholic Church teaches certain doctrines and dogmas as absolute truths that must be believed. Based on these doctrines, the Church determines what is good moral behavior and what is not. Growing up as a Catholic, I never questioned any of these teachings. I thought that, if I questioned them, I was in immediate danger of losing my faith. The possibility of eternal damnation due to losing my faith was enough to keep me trying to stay on the straight and narrow way.

As is evident from the previous chapters, I came to question a lot of what the Roman Catholic Church taught, realizing that I could be wrong. The certainty I had when just going along with what the Church taught is what was lost. Being true to my conscience and myself required living with uncertainty. To my surprise, I did not lose my faith. Rather, I found a deeper level of faith in taking responsibility for my beliefs, accepting the uncertainty, and just trying to be as trusting and open to our loving God as I could be. I no longer felt guilty about questioning Church teachings.

My stance may come across as having been arrogant, as though I thought I knew better than the Church; yet I had to follow my conscience. The teachings of Vatican Council II aimed at opening up the Church to a more open relationship with the modern world. Unfortunately, many in the Church hierarchy have worked for the last five decades to reverse the reforms envisioned by Vatican II and to suppress anything considered dissent.

Pope Francis is making a heroic effort to make the Roman Catholic Church a more merciful and compassionate spiritual home and to influence the hierarchy to be more open to change. However, he has been facing strong resistance from an entrenched conservative minority, especially in the Roman curia.

CHAPTER 9

My Creed

IN PREVIOUS CHAPTERS I MADE IT CLEAR that I strongly disagreed with the way Popes John Paul II and Benedict XVI exercised their authority in the Roman Catholic Church. Because I might not have been sufficiently clear about my specific disagreements, what follows is a discussion of some of the major areas where I came to believe that they were simply wrong. That may sound extremely arrogant, but I sincerely disagreed with them on the following issues.

First, I disagreed strongly with their teachings about lesbian, gay, bisexual, and transgender (LGBTQ+) people and the labeling of their relationships and sexual behavior as being "inherently evil" and "intrinsically disordered." As a result of these teachings, the Roman Catholic Church in America mounted expensive political campaigns to the tune of millions of dollars to block legalization of civil marriage between LGBTQ+ people. Gay persons will tell you that they do not choose to be gay; they are born with their gender orientation, just as heterosexuals are, even though it may differ from the physical anatomy they were born with. If God creates people that way, how can the Catholic Church discriminate against them?

I also opposed the rule of mandatory celibacy for the priesthood. In my view, this rule mainly serves to perpetuate a caste system that protects the clergy's power and status. At the very start of Christianity, St. Peter was married and, later, so were some of the popes and many priests until celibacy was mandated early in the 12th century. The long history of sexual scandals in the Church, and especially the recent revelations of sexual abuse of children by Roman Catholic priests vowed to celibacy, should alone be sufficient reason to eliminate the mandatory celibacy rule.

The discriminatory treatment of women by the hierarchy is another area where I strongly disagreed with Church policy. I believed that the Church needs to include women in leadership positions and decision-making at all organizational levels (from local faith communities or parishes to regional dioceses and the Roman curia), including the ordination of women to the diaconate and priesthood.

The Roman Catholic Church's current position in regard to women's ordination was put forth by Pope John Paul II and is treated as though it was an infallible teaching. There is historical evidence that women have been ordained, both in the early Church and in more recent times. It is important to note that the Pontifical Biblical Commission stated that there is nothing in Scripture that forbids the ordination of women.

The mere fact that a pope declares something as though it were infallible doesn't mean that it is, especially if he has not consulted the whole Church and met the theological requirements to do so. I believed that many theologians and bishops would agree that Pope John Paul II's document negating the ordination of women is not an infallible teaching. Both Popes John Paul II and Benedict XVI seemed to consider their personal beliefs to be Church doctrine without consulting their fellow Bishops and the faithful, the People of God.

During the papacy of Pope Benedict XVI, women religious in the United States who do so much to serve the poor were marginalized, suspected of not being loyal to church teachings, and investigated by the Vatican. This investigation came across to me as resulting more from some American bishops' pique about the sisters daring to publicly differ with them on health care and LGBTQ+ issues (among others), than from any real wrongdoing on the part of the sisters. Not surprisingly, the Vatican investigators found nothing amiss in the way the sisters were conducting themselves.

I found sexuality to be another area where the teaching authority of the Church has grave difficulty, and is way behind the times in relation to both current scientific knowledge and how it should inform moral theology. Pope Paul VI's 1968 encyclical *Humanae Vitae* condemned artificial birth control but was never well-received by many bishops, priests, and lay Catholics worldwide. Most priests don't preach against artificial birth control and it is estimated that over 80% of Catholics in America reject or ignore Pope Paul VI's decree against artificial birth control.

According to Catholic tradition, a rule is not valid unless and until it is accepted by the whole Church, including the laity. Many theologians disagree with the "official" Church teachings regarding sexuality and long for the day when reform/updating can be seriously considered. Theologians who have spoken out, like Father Charles Curran, have been silenced, disciplined and/or forbidden to teach in Catholic universities.

Father Curran taught moral theology for several years at the Catholic University of America in Washington, D.C. In 1986 he was informed by the Congregation of the Faith headed by Cardinal Joseph Ratzinger (later Pope Benedict XVI) that he was unfit to teach Catholic theology unless he recanted his teachings on sexual morality. He dissented from the Church's teachings on many sexual issues, such as contraception, and was the first Catholic theologian to support same-sex unions. Since he did not recant, he was fired by Catholic University. In 1991 he was hired as a tenured professor teaching Christian ethics at Southern Methodist University.

If there is an issue that polarizes the Catholic community more than any other, it is abortion. A common reaction of many Catholics to anyone who questions the Church's total ban against abortion is to brand that person as immoral, even as a murderer. Again, this is an area where not all theologians agree. I suspected that there were also some bishops who questioned the absolute ban against abortions, but didn't dare to do so openly in today's Church.

In past centuries the Church did not always ban all abortions. Because it is not known exactly when a fertilized embryo becomes a human person, the Church today bans abortion from the very moment of conception. This may not be something science can ever determine, but I didn't believe that an embryo becomes a human being at least until the heart starts beating.

I was basically pro-life and believed that human life should be respected and supported from conception to the end of life. It distressed me that avid "pro-life" people often seemed to have much less concern about the welfare of human beings from infancy through old age than about the fetus in the womb.

I also believed that abortion can be a moral choice to save the life of a mother, in cases of rape and incest, or in various circumstances that negatively affect the mother and her fetus. The circumstances or context surrounding an act do make a moral difference. And the Church's teaching concerning the primacy of the individual's conscience should allow a woman to make an informed choice about what happens to her own body.

I have also disagreed with Church teaching and practice regarding other issues, such as the treatment of divorced and remarried Catholics and the rules regarding the liturgy. And I have always acknowledged that I could be wrong.

A major disagreement I had with Church government concerned the silencing of all disagreement. If any person—whether cardinal, bishop, priest, theologian, religious, or lay person—voiced an opinion contrary to the "official" teaching of the Church, that person was considered to be not only disloyal, but often heretical. The official refusal to allow any discussion of issues, like those previously mentioned, seemed to me to be both spiritually unhealthy and theologically suspect. If the American experience has taught us anything, it is the importance of the right to free speech. Primacy of conscience, the right to follow one's conscience even when it is contrary to Church teaching, is too often ignored and not taught to the faithful.

This book has been an attempt to explain how I changed so drastically from the person I was through my nearly four decades of life regarding what I believed and how I related to God and other people. Intellectual beliefs may guide surface behavior, but the feelings underneath these beliefs are the real motivating factors. I was able to become free to love and grow only to the extent that I could come to grips with my negative feelings of fear, anger, hate, and envy— and become less judgmental. My beliefs changed over the years in relation to my growing awareness of the mystery of life. And I've spent my last days on earth looking forward to continued life in the hereafter, to the ongoing experience of an expanding awareness of God's infinite and unconditional love.

Some may question how I, an ordinary guy, could have questioned the doctrines that the Church teaches? There is a tendency is to identify our beliefs with our faith. What we believe about God affects our faith and our lives, but I came to understand that belief and faith are not identical. Our beliefs can change and, in many instances, should change as our understanding of God and reality deepens. As adults who take responsibility for what we believe, we need to question our beliefs.

Faith is different. Faith is our relationship with God. One may believe that God is waiting to punish every bad deed, or one may believe that God doesn't punish anyone. One may believe there is no God or that no one can know for sure if there is a God.

But faith is not an intellectual belief. Faith is a relationship. You can disagree strongly with another person and still have a good relationship with that person. So, faith and belief are not identical. Therefore, to question your beliefs does not mean that you are losing your faith, that is, your relationship with God.

On a positive note, the theology and spirituality that became most spiritually enriching for me in the last years of my life were what are often referred to as "evolutionary theology" and "creation spirituality." The thinking in these fields of knowledge is consistent with today's science. Current scientific knowledge is new and modern, but evolutionary theology is based on a traditional alternative orthodoxy. Yet it sounds like new theology because the Roman Catholic Church has basically ignored it in order to focus on creedal statements based on a fall/redemption theology.

Expressions of evolutionary theology and creation spirituality can be found in Scripture, particularly in the Gospels and Pauline letters. This alternative orthodoxy was taught by St. Francis of Assisi, St. Bonaventure and Blessed Duns Scotus in the Middle Ages. It is still lived and taught today by some Franciscans.

Evolutionary theologians study recent discoveries in physics and biology regarding the progression of life from the Big Bang to the present in order to better understand the increasing complexity of creation, our relationship with our Creator God, and our purpose on earth. In particular, they study how human beings evolved to have the capacities of thought, reflection and free will—the only creatures who not only know but know that they know.

Evolution proceeds from matter to spirit, with the universe becoming ever more conscious of itself. What made this exciting to me was that neither evolution nor God's creativity in this process is finalized. Because of humanity's growing, evolving consciousness, we are in the process of becoming more essential and influential participants (or co-creators) in the future direction of evolution.

The writings of Teilhard de Chardin began to bring together theology and evolutionary science. He was silenced by the Church and died in 1955. Since Vatican Council II his writings have been rescued and continue to influence modern theology. Many other authors have advanced aspects of evolutionary theology and creation spirituality in their writings, including Thomas Berry, Brian Swimme, Michael Dowd, Matthew Fox, Michael Morwood, Thomas Merton, Ilia Deleo and Diarmid O'Murchu.

Richard Rohr, a well-known Franciscan priest and author, is especially good at applying evolutionary theology to the spiritual life. He also relies on the writings of the Christian mystics, such as Meister Eckhart, St. Teresa of Avila, Julian of Norwich, and St. Hildegarde of Bingen.

Evolutionary theology and creation spirituality (in contrast to the fall/redemption theology that is the core of so much Church teaching) gave me—a laicized, married Catholic priest—a very different perspective on the nature and meaning of God, creation, and our relationship with the modern world. In particular, it strengthened my belief in a God of love.

Genesis tells us that we are created in God's image and likeness. But what does this mean? I came to believe that human beings are most godlike when they are expressing unconditional love. God gave mankind the gift of free will. We can freely love or freely decide to make selfish choices. Because God gave us free will, God cannot act against or violate our free will.

We often ask why God allows evil as we observe both loving kindness and mankind's inhumanity to fellow humans on a daily basis. God responds with love but does not intervene or force anyone to love and avoid evil. God does not intervene in human affairs today any more than He/She did to prevent the crucifixion of Jesus. God does not punish. God only loves. I came to believe that sin is its own punishment because of its consequences for the sinner. As Jesus said when he hung on the cross, "Father, forgive them for they know not what they do." God cannot intervene without violating our free will; therefore, God does not intervene.

Summary of My Beliefs

I believed in Jesus, the Risen Christ, the Anointed One. I believed in the Trinity. I believed in evolutionary theology. I believed in the Church as the People of God, the Mystical Body of Christ.

I loved participating in sacred liturgies. I especially loved my wife, my children, and my grandchildren. I loved and treasured all the friends I ever had. I believed in the new cosmology and that the universe is 13.8 billion years old. I believed that the Bible is God's word, but not as a literal translation. I believed in reincarnation. I believed in God's great mercy and kindness and eternal love. I believed that nature is God's first revelation and that the earth and the entire universe are sacred.

I believed in equality and inclusivity and opposed discrimination in any form, including discrimination based on religion, race, country of origin, education, sexual orientation, or socioeconomic status. I believed that the theology concerning sexuality, as traditionally taught by the Roman Catholic Church, is very screwed up (pun intended) and out of line with emerging scientific knowledge and moral theology. The existence (or not) of a loving relationship has to be one of the major criteria for judging any behavior. I believed in a couple's right to practice responsible contraception and in a woman's right to choose abortion in certain cases.

I believed that those who practice other religions are not less religious or pleasing to God simply because they worship and identify God by a different name, or if their beliefs and religious/spiritual practices differ from mine. I also believed that people who do not belong to any particular religion (or identify themselves as atheists or agnostics), but live lives that exemplify positive values of love and justice, are in a good relationship with God.

I believed that the Divine Presence is everywhere and in everything—that everything is sacred and God is always with us and in us. Therefore, I also believed that the Golden Rule applies to everyone.

Richard Rohr has reminded us in his writings that we can only know God through metaphor. For example, one metaphor conceives of God as the ocean and we humans as fish in that ocean. Fish can only live and survive in the ocean and we can only live and survive in God. The ocean metaphor helps us to realize that the immense, vast ocean in which we live, and move, and have our being every day of our lives is an ocean of Divine Love.

I longed for the full implementation of the Second Vatican Council documents but didn't really expect to live to see this. I found it hopeful that Pope Francis' approach to his leadership role has been less concerned with church law and more concerned with pastoral ministry. However, despite his efforts to focus the Roman Catholic Church on manifesting the Gospel message of love, mercy, compassion, and inclusion, Pope Francis has not been able to bring about any significant change in the Church's position in areas such as the status of women in the Church or the Church's moral theology and rules concerning sexuality.

I was an ordinary guy and could be angry, selfish, lazy, lustful, proud, and deceitful like anyone else. I forgave anyone who ever hurt or offended me and I was deeply sorry for any hurt or offense I ever caused anyone else. I just kept trying to follow Jesus and live each day in a spirit of gratitude and joy. After being so spiritually rigid in my early years, I finally felt tremendously free—free to be me, the son of a fantastic Father/Mother/Creator God and brother of Jesus, in happy relationships with my extraordinary wife, family and friends, and one with all of mankind. And I looked forward to one hell of an exciting future on the other side!

AL'S EPILOGUE

AFTER I SHARED THE PREVIOUS CHAPTER WITH an authors' group to which I belonged, it was suggested that I write more concerning my ideas about God. I immediately thought of a quote from Greg Braden's book, *The God Code:*

> In recent years some scientists have suggested that our modern world has outgrown the need for spirituality-based explanations of life's mysteries. In the German news magazine Der Spiegel, renowned theoretical physicist Stephen Hawking illustrated this viewpoint when he stated, "What I have done is to show that it is possible for the way the universe began to be determined by the laws of science. . . . This doesn't prove that there is no God, only that God is not necessary." Recent discoveries in the rapidly evolving field of quantum physics now suggest that Hawking's "laws of science" and the "God" of spiritual traditions may, in fact, be related in surprising and unexpected ways. Ultimately, we may discover that they are references to precisely the same force![1]

---

[1] *Greg Braden. The God Code: The Secret of Our Past the Promise of Our Future (Carlsbad, CA: Hay House, Inc., 2004), 155.*

This is not the place to go deeply into quantum physics, but the recent discoveries in this field are both surprising and exciting. For example, physicists have discovered that spatial distance has no effect on the relationship between elemental particles. In an experiment, physicists cut a particle in two and separated the two particle halves by thirteen miles. They then spun one of the particle halves. To their surprise, the other particle half thirteen miles away spun spontaneously at the same time.

The scientists called this result "quantum entanglement", the ability of separated objects to share a condition or state. They are connected and not independent of one another no matter how far apart they are. Einstein called it "spooky action at a distance."

Such a quantum field is not material; it is an energy field. One conclusion from the scientific evidence of quantum entanglement is that evolution's dictum "survival of the fittest" is, perhaps, less responsible for evolution's trends than the relationship and cooperation of particles on the elemental level.

Physicists today, whether atheist or not, believe that matter has a non-material or energy aspect. For example, note the equal sign in Einstein's famous formula $E = mc$ squared. Braden concluded that his "God Code" research findings indicate that the name of God is written into our very DNA.

There is no scientific proof that God exists and there probably never will be. Scientists believe that they deal only with what is measurable and quantifiable. Spiritual realms are considered to be outside their field of study.

So, the scientist, as a scientist, does not comment on spiritual, non-material things that can't be measured. Some scientists decide to approach the spiritual realm as agnostics or atheists. Other scientists do, in fact, believe in God.

A scientist can look at a beautiful sunset and explain how it is caused by the reflection of light on the clouds and how light contains all colors of the spectrum. I looked at sunsets and saw great beauty that left me in awe of nature. My knowledge about sunsets was not scientific. It was experiential. Another person could argue that I was wrong because they perceive sunsets as being ugly. They are entitled to their opinion. The point is that everyone has experiential knowledge. That is where I discovered God. The discoveries of science—and especially those of quantum physics—also left me in awe.

What about us ordinary guys? Who hasn't at some time in their life questioned the existence of God or at least complained, "Why me?" How can a loving God permit so much suffering, harm, and injustice in the world? If God permeates and sustains, not only each human person, but every part of the entire universe, how come we have such terrible natural disasters? These are the questions almost everyone asks. . . and they are the wrong questions. They betray a misunderstanding of God and of who we are.

It is so easy to misunderstand God. We humans are constrained by the limits of our human language, culture, and intelligence. Do we expect a fly to understand a human being? Why then do we expect a human being to be able to understand God? The difference is so vast. God remains a mystery to us no matter how much we try to understand Him/Her. It's like the story of the ten blind men each touching a different part of an elephant thinking they then know and understand the whole elephant.

The Bible says that we are made in the image of God. The problem is that we tend to imagine God in our own image. Thus, we use the he/she/it pronouns for a genderless Divine Being. We imagine God as an all-powerful ruler able to do anything He/She wants. We anthropomorphize God, most often imagining God as an old man with a beard sitting on a throne waiting to judge us and, perhaps, condemn us to hell—especially if we have not honored Him often enough and appropriately enough.

Therefore, we often perceive God as someone to be feared, rather than as an infinitely-loving and compassionate Divine Presence. However, God is not to be feared. Scripture says that, "Fear of the Lord is the beginning of Wisdom." (Psalm 111:10; Proverb 1:7. Sirach 1:72.) But, today, some scripture scholars propose that a better translation for the word "fear" in these Scripture passages is "reverence" or "awe." This passage then would then be read as: "Reverence for God" or "Awe of God" is the beginning of wisdom.

The problem is that we cannot know God the same way we humans come to know everything else—through our normal human senses. But, in the silence of contemplation, we can open ourselves to experience God directly, without words/God to soul, like the mystics in every religious tradition have done. This fulfills the first great commandment to love God with your whole heart, soul and mind.

The second way we experience God is through our relationships with our fellow humans, especially when we offer each other unconditional love. Humans are most god-like (most true to their being created in the Divine Image) when they express unconditional love for each other. This fulfills the second great commandment: To love your neighbor as yourself. As mentioned before, physicists have discovered a relationship that exists between elemental particles despite space separation. In like manner, we humans are related to each other, connected to each other despite spatial separation or the perceived differences that so often separate us (e.g., race, religion, ethnicity, social class, gender, etc.).

Discovering the God of the Universe brought me great joy. I came to know God as sheer love, an infinitely loving life force. Richard Rohr has described God as "a divine Trinitarian dance of loving relationships."[1] The universe is seen as resulting from an explosion (the Big Bang), as an expression of God in time and space.

Not that God is the universe, but that the universe is an expression of God, as are we. God is in every bit of it. The universe is an expression of God's free and unconditional love with no strings attached.

For us intelligent, conscious human beings to express love, we have to be free. It is not love, especially not unconditional love, unless the love is freely given. Thus, we can choose to love or to make selfish, hateful choices. The evil in the world is not from God. We humans create our own evil.

---

[1] *Richard Rohr. The Divine Dance: The Trinity and Your Transformation (New Kensington, PA: Whitaker House, 2004), 27.*

What about the tragedies in the world—the natural disasters that we do not cause and cannot avoid? Even then, as the scientists tell us, nothing is lost. And death always precedes new life. Doesn't this "loss and renewal" law of science also apply to human life? Part of the mystery of life is that our deaths precede new life for us. If we have learned to love in this life, we die into a greater love. If we die full of hate and evil, we have prepared ourselves for a not so happy future with a lot of learning to do on the other side.

We experience God whenever we love unselfishly and whenever we are open to receiving love. That is the case whether we are aware of it or not. "Dark nights of the soul" are experienced by some as periods when no sensory consolations are experienced and we are tempted to doubt God. Probably every believer experiences them to some extent. Theresa of Calcutta and John of the Cross were saints who loved God greatly but experienced long periods of spiritual dryness, not feeling any spiritual consolation. They questioned God, but continued to live lives dedicated to love of God and neighbor.

What follows are a couple of quotations that exemplify the experiential knowledge of God described by the mystics. The first example is from Mechtild of Magdeburg (1212-1281):

The day of my spiritual awakening
was the day I saw
and knew that I saw
all things in God
and God in all things.

Mechtild didn't read this in a book or hear it in church. She saw and knew she saw—all things in God and God in all things.

A second example of experiential knowledge of God was expressed by Blessed Angela of Foligno, a 13th century Franciscan penitent, mystic and teacher of theologians. She said she experienced the world as "pregnant with God."

Although these are examples are from medieval mystics, we all can have access to experiential knowing. It is up to the individual to decide how truthful or believable that knowledge is for them.

I BELIEVED IN GOD

Saying that I believed in God means I believed intellectually that God exists. But I also believed God directly, experientially—meaning that we had an ongoing relationship. I believed that God touched my being and communicated directly with me. I was not special because of this. Everyone is in relationship with God whether they are aware of it or not. God not only created us in the first place but sustains us in every moment of our existence—otherwise we would cease to exist. St. Paul expressed this reality in a speech he gave to the people of Athens: "For in him we live and move and have our being." (Acts 17:28)

My understanding of God changed over the years. In my early years I thought of God as an authority figure, somewhat like a stern Santa Claus, waiting to see if I was going to be naughty or nice—only the consequences were upped a bit. Being naughty would merit eternal damnation in hell. Fear of hell was probably what primarily motivated my behavior for the first 35 years of my life.

As I matured, I came to understand that God is not Santa Claus. Nor is God even a person in the human sense. I believed that "Divine Presence" describes God more realistically. The Divine Presence is every-where, permeates every bit of the entire cosmos, and sustains the existence of everything, both ani-mate and inanimate.

Another way of saying this is to describe God as the Life Force, the infinitely loving flow of energy that sustains all matter and all life. The fecundity of life surrounds us: for example, the little twig of grass that sprouts up between cracks in the cement. Given a chance, living things sprout up, grow, and survive everywhere—even in difficult circumstances.

I believed in the Divine Presence as far back as I can remember. I felt that I was always within the Divine Presence and never felt alone. And I have never felt that I could hide from that Presence. When the circumstances of my life changed in my thirties, I began to question everything I believed about God; yet I never questioned the reality of an infinitely loving Divine Presence.

I came to believe that God is not capable of punishing anyone because God loves everyone too much. After all, God created each one of us. God also gave each one of us the free will that enables us to choose to be as god-like or as god-less as we wish. God will never take away or violate our free will; thus, humans can punish others by acting on cruel and harmful choices or they can act god-like by choosing to love others unconditionally.

I preferred to think that I believed God rather than that I believed in God. To believe in God is an activity of the intellect, whereas to believe God directly puts me in relationship with God. That relationship required that I be open to receiving God's unconditional love.

A unique feature of unconditional love is that it cannot be earned or deserved in any way. The only response I knew was to gratefully say 'thank you' and pass on that unconditional love to others. As the 13th century mystic Meister Eckhart (1260 – 1328) said, "If the only prayer you ever say in your life is 'thank you', it will be enough." Or as Dag Hammarskjold expressed it: "For all that has been, thanks. To all that shall be, Yes."

I couldn't offer any proof that the God I believed in really exists. I would have understood if someone told me they thought my belief was delusional and flowed from an overactive religious imagination. I believed that I experienced God's love when I received unconditional love from another person. I couldn't touch or feel God with my human senses, yet I knew I that I experienced the Divine Presence.

How could I describe that love relationship? The closest description I could give was the way I felt when I fell in love with my wife. Suddenly I felt like my feet didn't touch the ground. I was ecstatic to find myself loved unconditionally and not because I deserved it or had done anything to receive such love. What a fantastic feeling! I wanted to love my wife in return and do anything she might ask of me.

Everything was right in my world. I just wanted us to be happy together.

I believed with all my heart that the Divine Presence permeates the entire cosmos, expressing "Godness" with the sheer force of an infinitely-loving energy that cares about every bit or particle of creation, including each and every one of us.

Father Richard Rohr reminds his readers that God is not a noun—God is a verb. Like Father Richard, I believed that God is not someone waiting to be adored and worshipped. God is too busy expressing love for all creation and sustaining everything in existence.

It felt so wonderful to know that I was a part of this awesome cosmos and part of the human race (the People of God, Christ's mystical Body). I knew that I belonged and I was not alone. That was the kind of feeling I had when I was aware of being in the presence of the constant flow of Divine Love. As St. Augustine stated in his *Confessions,* "God is closer to us than we are to ourselves."

I was convinced that nothing that happens can ever take that relationship away from me. I could revel in that Divine Presence and enjoy it. I could feel Love no matter my circumstances. For example, I could be in physical pain or upset and terribly worried over my life circumstances, yet I could still be happy and hopeful. As the mystic, Julian of Norwich (1342 – 1416) reassured us, ". . . all shall be well, all shall be well, and all manner of things shall be well."

This final paragraph summarizes the "journey to joy" I have lived and have been describing in this book.

LOUISE'S EPILOGUE

A S MENTIONED IN THE PREFACE TO THIS edition of *Journey to Joy: From Spiritual Rigidity to Freedom*, one of the main reasons for preparing this 2nd edition was to tell the story of how Al's earthly "journey to joy" ended; to tell how he lived by his personal creed through the joys and life challenges he faced during the last two decades of his life, and how he transformed them into opportunities to grow in love and grace.

Before stories about Al's life in retirement are told to round out the story he presented in the first edition of his spiritual autobiography, the next section presents my sense of how the metaphor of "Falling Upwards" (eloquently described by Father Richard Rohr in his book with the same name) throws light on Al's pre-retirement years. Based on the work of Swiss psychologist Carl Jung (1875-1971), Father Richard describes two halves of life: the first half is the survival dance that most of us think is our primary task in life, while the second half of life entails getting beyond our survival dance and into our sacred dance, moving beyond ego questions of security and success to questions of the soul.

Chapters Two through Six of Al's autobiography primarily describe how the survival dance of the first half of his life evolved. Growing up in a very religious and rule-bound German Roman Catholic family in the Midwest helped young Ronald Albert to build a strong identity (or container for his life). It provided security, order, and consistency. But it also produced in him a fear of evil and the possibility of going to hell that impelled him to enter Maryknoll and start preparation for priestly ordination as soon as he finished high school. Despite a few setbacks (like his difficulty with learning Latin!) the nine years of his seminary training continued his development of a strong identity and career direction as well as providing a broadening of his social relationships.

The ten years of his missionary life as a Maryknoll priest in South Korea had their challenges, especially learning the Korean language and customs. Al really enjoyed ministering to the mostly rural flocks he tended and his part in the successful establishment of a pig cooperative that raised the living standards of many poor farm families.

Then Vatican Council II happened. The teachings contained in the 16 Council documents required radical changes in the Roman Catholic Church worldview and practices, especially those regarding: 1) the Church being made up of the whole People of God and operating according to the principles of solidarity with all of the People of God by virtue of their baptismal priesthood, with not just the hierarchy having a voice in decision-making; 2) the encouragement of ecumenism in relationship to other religions; and 3) the liturgies being performed in the vernacular of each world region (rather than universally in Latin), the Mass celebrated with the priest facing the people and with the laity's active participation throughout the liturgy, and the offering of both bread and wine to the faithful at communion time.

As Al explained in Chapter Four, he was profoundly affected by Vatican Council II. It led him to question the teachings, rules, and regulations of the Church that he had accepted without question since boyhood. He loved that Pope John XXIII, through initiating this Council, had brought about a profound opening up of the Church to new ways of thinking about and relating to the modern world. However, it also led to his becoming angry about many in the Church hierarchy, and even some of his fellow Maryknollers, who did not fully accept the changes.

During this difficult time period, Al started opening up and transitioning to the challenges of the second half of life. He had to grapple with the difficult decision to leave Maryknoll and the priesthood, and to resume lay life at age 38 without financial security or a sure career path. As he went through this painful more-than-a-year-long process, Dr. Whitmont (the Jungian psychiatrist) helped him to get in touch with his feelings for the first time in his life and begin to process the anger issues which had played a big part in his leaving the priesthood.

This meant that Al was opening up to stretching and doing repair work on his container (his identity) so it could stretch enough to hold "new wine" for the sacred dance of his second half of life. Al still had to be largely in the survival dance mode of the first half of life because of his late start in pursuing security and success according to social norms for an American male. He was fortunate to secure a position as a youth counselor which was very helpful during that year of transition.

Then Al met me and our rather whirlwind courtship and marriage added to Al's first half of life challenges—learning the new role of being a good husband. His unconditional love for me met that challenge as we grew to know and love each other more day by day. The biggest impetus to his continuing his transition to the sacred dance of the second half of life occurred during my first and only pregnancy: learning that the baby I was carrying (and which we wanted very much) had a serious genetic abnormality.

The agonizing process we went through in deciding to terminate the pregnancy (as described in Chapter One) put a huge strain on our marriage. But our belief in the Church's doctrine of the primacy of the individual conscience, the reassurance we found in the teachings of contemporary moral theologians we respected, and our reluctance to bring into the world a child we believed would face a very short and difficult life, helped us to be at peace with our decision and move on, despite the devastating feelings of grief and loss we both experienced.

According to Father Richard, the transition from the first to the second half of life is not something that we can engineer ourselves. It is done to us—and it takes trust to fall and not fall apart. Al went through this "falling" process again early in our married life when, after we moved from New York back to Massachusetts, he started a promising career as a family and youth therapist. Al was unfairly accused by a client and, as a result, lost his license to practice as a therapist.

Thus, I became the major family breadwinner during the rest of our marriage. Al had to follow my university teaching position changes and find a new career path in Massachusetts, then in Wisconsin, and finally in Southern California.

This situation certainly challenged the identity container Al had developed in his first half of life, since it didn't fit male cultural norms for success in American society. It was not easy for him, but he handled the situation with inner strength and maturity. The strong ego structure he had built in his first half of life enabled him to deal with this situation steadfastly through the years of parenting our girls and my ongoing academic career.

When we were looking for a place to live in the San Diego area in 1989, the rental agent we were dealing with mentioned an opportunity that I thought might, at last, give Al a chance to have some solid career success in a business he was well-qualified to undertake. The rental agent told us about a woman who was looking for a buyer for her educational tutoring business located in a nearby Solana Beach, California mall. Al took over The Educational Tutoring Center and things got off to a good start.

The following year the United States experienced the 1990 recession. Many parents who had

previously sought tutoring to help their children succeed in school could no longer afford to do so. Al
ultimately had to give up the business and we had
to file for bankruptcy. This turn of events was very
painful for both of us. I had so much wanted Al to
experience success in this career endeavor.

Al's faith, and his love for God and for me and
the girls, helped him to navigate the many career
challenges he faced during those years in a way
that helped him to "fall upward", to continue
his transition to the sacred dance of the second
half of his life, further opening himself up to the
opportunities for spiritual growth that marked his
later years.

Move to Nevada

In 2000 Al and I were still living in San Diego and
I was still teaching in the School of Nursing at the
University of San Diego (USD). But both of our daughters and their families were living in Henderson,
Nevada in the southeast part of the Las Vegas valley.
Ann and her husband Jim had been dropping hints
about our possibly moving up there to be nearer to
them during our retirement years. The idea grew
on us, especially after we realized how much less
the cost of living would be in Nevada compared with
Southern California.

When we toured the Sun City Anthem Over-55
Community on one of our visits to Henderson, we
became convinced that this would be a good move
for us. So, we signed on the dotted line to have a

house built on a lot that gave us a view of Mount Charleston. This was important because Al loved mountains!

We had never had a house built before and it was exciting to watch the progress in its construction on successive trips from San Diego to Henderson. Our granddaughter Sara, who was about four at the time, enjoyed visiting the construction site and claimed the second bedroom as her own (although she never actually slept in it after construction was completed).

Once move-in time arrived in Spring 2001, I was still teaching in San Diego so I could only spend vacation times and long weekends in our new home. But Al was already fully retired. He made our new house in Sun City Anthem his main residence and I downsized from a house to a condominium unit in San Diego until I retired from my faculty position in 2003.

Al really enjoyed living in our new home and considered it his "man cave." He enjoyed walking up and down the Las Vegas Strip, playing video poker in the casinos now and then, as well as handicapping horse races. After I retired in May 2003 and moved into our new home full-time, Al was happy to have me living there with him 24/7. But he never really got over my cluttering up his "man cave" with all my stuff! We had lots of fun working out the details of furnishing our new home together and exploring the many amenities offered by our Sun City Anthem community.

Senior Theatre Involvement

In early Fall 2003 I discovered that the University of Nevada Las Vegas Senior Adult Theatre Program (UNLVSATP) was offering an acting course at our Sun City Anthem community center. This reminded me of the fun I had in high school performing in plays and variety shows.

So, I signed up for the class, never dreaming that Al would soon accidentally become involved in theatre performance as well. He had never expressed any interest in performing and was born under the astrological sign of Libra. In addition, Al was an introvert according to the Myers-Briggs Personality Test.

I also tended toward introversion, but was born under the sign of Leo. Since Leo's are said to love the limelight, maybe this is why I have enjoyed performing and entertaining others so much.

During that first UNLVSATP class, students were encouraged to audition for a part in a one-act play festival to take place at UNLV in early 2004. I memorized a monologue, auditioned, and got a part in a one-act play entitled *Gennifer*.

Al and I attended a church meeting a few weeks later, after which he came with me to the theater on the UNLV campus where an early rehearsal of *Gennifer* was scheduled. Al expected to sit in the last row of the theater and read or take a nap during the rehearsal. However, the fellow who had been cast as my husband in the play had had to drop out. So, when the director of the play saw Al come in into the theatre with me, he exclaimed: "Don't sit down; come down here onto the stage!"

What followed was a spontaneous audition for the part of my husband in the play. Al was offered the part and, after thinking it over, he accepted it. This was the start of almost 20 wonderful years of Al and I performing together in plays and variety shows throughout the Las Vegas valley.

During one of the UNLVSATP acting courses we took together, Al played the role of Jerry, a jazz bass player, in a scene from *Some Like It Hot* (the role played by Jack Lemon in the movie). To escape Chicago mob retaliation, Jerry and his friend Joe (played by Tony Curtis in the movie) disguised themselves as female musicians, Daphne and Josephine, and joined an all-female band on a train headed for Miami. Both of them became obsessed with Sugar (played by Marilyn Monroe in the film) and had to struggle to remember not to make passes at her because they were supposed to be girls.

I had the fun of helping Al get his Daphne role costume together. Luckily, I had a black satin tent dress with big white polka dots and broad shoulders (inherited from my stepmother) that was big enough to fit him, as well as a light brown woman's wig and some torturous panty hose. The trickiest item to get was a pair of dress heels to fit his wide width, 11-12 men's shoe size feet. What a sight he was sitting in the women's shoe department of the local Nordstrom's Rack store: a six foot guy with broad shoulders sitting there trying on women's dress shoes! We even had the good fortune to find a pair that fit!.

When the instructor, Doug Hill, saw Al gussied up in his Daphne costume at the next rehearsal of the scene, he exclaimed that he had never seen a homelier woman! And the actress who played Sugar in the scene had a very hard time keeping a straight face. Al was a very good sport all through this ordeal, but was very happy to take off that uncomfortable costume for the last time.

A major highlight for Al during our years with the UNLVSATP was his performance of a very funny monologue he wrote about not wanting to marry a nurse or a teacher or an ex-nun—and then meeting and marrying me, despite my representing all of his triple bossiness no-nos!! He was so eager to perform this monologue in the UNLV theater that he passed up a trip to the Canadian Rockies! I had to invite our old friend Gail Baggot from Andover, Massachusetts to go with me instead.

In 2011, after UNLV discontinued the SATP following the 2008 recession, Al and I were founding members of The Speeding Theatre—Over 55, the only independent, nonprofit senior theatre company in the State of Nevada. Over the next decade we especially enjoyed shortening episodes of the very funny 1950s *The Bickersons* radio shows to four or five minute segments. Then we "bickered through" them in many variety shows that senior audiences really enjoyed.

Al was a cast member in several full-length play productions, including *Lemonade and Pluto* and *Golf with Alan Shepard.* His final play appearance took place five months before his passing. At age 89 he played a 95 year-old rabbi in *Jack Benny Isn't 39 Anymore.* He grew a beard for the role and was brought on and off stage in a wheelchair. (This was a perfect role for him since, at this point, Al could no longer walk unassisted.) The script specified that the rabbi keep falling asleep as the Jewish mother tries to get him to advise her daughter against a mixed marriage. Al's favorite line was delivered when the mother shook him to wake him up: "Gott in Himmel!! What am I, a salt-shaker?" After the play run, Al trimmed his beard but kept it so he wouldn't have to go back to shaving.

It was a real blessing that Al and I had the opportunity to engage in these senior theatre activities together during our retirement years. They presented many opportunities to challenge ourselves to be creative, to try new ways of portraying roles, and to memorize lines—when it was so much harder to do so than when we were younger.

Personality-wise I never dreamed that Al would enjoy performing and perform so well in the senior theatre activities we shared. I consider it a bit of a miracle that added a lot of spice to our retirement years.

Other Retirement Activities

Al and I did a fair amount of traveling during the 20 years of our retirement. Our first trip in

Fall 2003 was a gift from daughter Ann and son-in-law Jim: an Alaska cruise. We boarded ship in Vancouver and enjoyed the wildlife, the native American cultural sites, the Gold Rush area tours, and the awesome sights in Glacier Bay when huge chunks of ice fell off into the water. A helicopter ride to the top of the Mendenhall Glacier was another special treat that enabled us to step onto a glacier and look down into the awesome crevices of blue ice.

Al and Louise on Alaska Cruise, Fall 2003

Family Trip to Hawaii, 2014
From Left to Right: Lisa, Andrew, Sara, Ann, Al & Louise

In 2010 we enjoyed a Panama Canal cruise and in 2013 a Rhone River cruise in France. A family trip to Hawaii in 2014 with Ann and Lisa and their families celebrated my upcoming 80th birthday and our 43rd wedding anniversary. Over these two decades we also had a trip to Glacier National Park in Montana and enjoyable car trips to Sedona and Flagstaff, Arizona, Albuquerque, New Mexico, and various venues in Northern and Southern California.

In his free time Al loved to read books on evolutionary theology and creation spirituality, as well as mystery novels. He would spend hours putting jigsaw puzzles together and handicapping the major horse races throughout the year. Al enjoyed placing modest bets on these horse races and occasionally visited a casino to play a little video poker. He was never a big winner in either of these activities but he was also never a big loser. For him, it was just good entertainment.

Al grew up in a large card-playing family and loved to play any kind of card game. We played Hand and Foot almost every evening after dinner. This is a type of canasta where you are dealt two hands (a Hand and a Foot) which are played sequentially. We also often played this game with other couples before or after enjoying a meal together. When we went over to Ann and Jim's house, we'd often have fun playing a card game called Oh, Hell! or (as our son-in-law Jim Petty called it) Petty Bridge.

Al put his training in priestly ministry—as well as the wisdom he gleaned from many years of spiritual reading, reflection, and prayer—to good use in offering "pro bono" spiritual direction to several friends we had made at church. As described in Chapter Seven of this book, he also had readings with Suzanne, our intuitive/medium friend and then spent time reflecting on the meaning of what came up during those sessions.

From 2016 to 2018 Al spent many hours writing drafts of his book chapters, and many more hours discussing the edits and re-writes suggested to him by me and by friends who read drafts and gave feedback. He attended the meetings of the Anthem

Authors Club in the Sun City Anthem community center where he read sections of his book drafts, and received suggestions for improvement from the group members—several of whom were well-established, published authors.

Al loved to complain to anyone who would listen about his perception that I paid more attention to correcting his grammar and punctuation slip-ups than focusing on the meaning he was trying to convey. I made it a point not to use red ink in making suggestions for change on his manuscript drafts since this seemed to make my feedback more difficult for him to accept.

If I could have afforded college after high school graduation, I would most likely have majored in English and been an English teacher. So, maybe there is still some of that "English teacher" in me after all these years. But I really did try to give Al helpful feedback concerning the meaning of his writings, as well as about his grammar and punctuation!

Another activity that was very important to Al was sending contributions to worthy charitable, social justice, and political causes. He took care of this until around 2019, when he was no longer able to write out the checks himself. So, we had to do this task together.

Despite the fact that a Vedic astrologer had assured me that I would never have a real problem financially, I was still a child of the depression in the 1930s. I found it difficult to write hundreds of dollars in checks at a time to so many different organizations. But Al calmly insisted that we needed to share what we could with nonprofit causes we believed in.

Al and I decided together which organizations we would contribute to, either quarterly or once or twice a year, made a list of them, and checked off every time a contribution was made. This helped me to get into the swing of things and actually enjoy knowing that our small contributions were helping to serve the needy and further good social causes. Since Al passed away in 2022, I am faithfully carrying on this effort in his memory.

Starting in Fall 2020 and early 2021 the Covid-19 epidemic added to the health issues Al and I faced, as it did to everyone else across the country and the world. Thanks to our avoidance of unnecessary contact with the outside world, our receiving of the Covid-19 vaccine and boosters as recommended by the CDC, and wearing masks when we ventured outside, neither Al nor I contracted Covid-19. The only weekly social event in our lives during that year and a half was a ten minute trip to our daughter Ann's home for a family dinner and, perhaps, a game or two of Petty Bridge on Sundays.

Early in the pandemic we decided to adopt a dog. We had been without a pet for a few years since our 22 year-old cat, Maizey, had died. I sensed that Al wanted me to have a canine companion for company because he expected to die before me. Many people were isolating themselves and working from home during that time, and lots of these folks were adopting pets, too. So, there were very few adoptable dogs in the local shelters.

We were fortunate to adopt a stray 19 pound, five-year-old, female miniature poodle/bichon frisee mix from the Las Vegas Animal Foundation. Maggie turned out to be a very lovable, easy to care for canine companion. Al and I both enjoyed having her in our lives. I loved taking her for walks around our neighborhood with Al along for the ride in his motor-ized chair. Since Al passed away, I have enjoyed, even more, having her as my "welcome committee" when I come home to an otherwise too quiet household.

Al holding Maggie, Spring 2022

Daughter Lisa surprised us when she called from San Diego in Summer 2021 to ask whether our grandson Andrew could live with us while attending

Nevada State College that Fall. Of course, we were delighted to say "Yes!" Andrew spent just that one semester with us because he decided to move back to San Diego and pursue a different educational path.

Al and I both enjoyed the opportunity to get to know Andrew better. Andrew is a shrewd card player and Al got him to play cards with us as often as he could spare the time to do so. Lisa's visits during the pandemic were few and far between. But, when she did visit, she would drive to a Korean market in Las Vegas and prepare a wonderful feast of Korean dishes that the whole family enjoyed together.

In 2021 granddaughter Sara became engaged to Gabriel Martin, a jazz musician she met while majoring in music performance at Chapman University in Orange, California. After spending most of the pandemic in Dallas, Texas, Sara and Gabe moved to Los Angeles and she earned a masters' degree in music performance at the University of Southern California (USC). She is currently enrolled in a doctoral program at USC and plans to both perform and teach music when she finishes the program.

During Spring 2022 Ann was kept busy helping Sara to plan and prepare for her May 29th wedding. Sara chose to be married in the same venue in Sun City Anthem where Al and I had celebrated our 50th wedding anniversary the year before. It meant a lot to Sara and the whole family that Al survived long enough to share in this joyous occasion!

Sara and Gabriel Martin's Wedding, 5/29/2023
Louise and Al with the newly married couple

Our Faith Community Transition

When Al and I moved to Henderson, Nevada we chose to join Christ the King Catholic Community in Las Vegas because it was the most Vatican Council II-oriented parish in the Las Vegas diocese—thanks to the tone set by its pastor, Father Bill Kenny. We were an active part of that parish for about 12 or 13 years. I served as a lector and tried to make the Word of God come alive in the way I presented the scripture readings to the congregation during weekly Masses. And, for a short time, I was also a member of the parish council.

Over those years Al became more and more dependent on using a walker due to increasing leg weakness, right knee instability, and loss of balance. It eventually became too difficult for him to traverse the long walk on uneven pavement from the nearest car drop-off point to the entrance to the church. So, we started to attend an Independent Catholic faith community that held liturgies in a much-easier-to-access storefront space.

What the heck is an Independent Catholic Church you ask? The main difference between an Independent Catholic Church and the Roman Catholic Church is that the former is self-governing and not under the jurisdiction of the Pope. The liturgy and sacraments practiced in Independent Catholic Churches are very similar to those in the Roman Catholic Church. In addition, Independent Catholic Churches, like the Roman Catholic Church, adhere to apostolic succession in the ordination of priests: the uninterrupted transmission of spiritual authority from the Apostles through successive popes and bishops.

Al and I resonated positively with the fact that the St. Marguerite Faith Community we joined is inclusive, regardless of one's marital status, gender identity, race, or other human distinctions that so often lead to exclusion. We also resonated positively with the faith community's profession of a more progressive evolutionary theology, the ordination of women and married persons, and the welcoming of divorced persons and the LGBTQ+ community in the life of the church.

It was not easy for us to leave the Roman Catholic Church we had grown up in, loved deeply, and been an active part of for so many years. However, we also felt that we could no longer support a church that excluded so many and would not allow any but a celibate male priesthood. We knew that many women, including St. Therese of Lisieux, have felt called to priesthood and many priests who left the active priesthood and married would love to have been allowed to continue to exercise priestly ministry in a Church faced with a rapidly declining number of priests. But systemic clericalism has put both the Roman Catholic hierarchy and its priests on a pedestal that offers career benefits many are loathe to give up.

We liked knowing that the pastor of St. Marguerite's was a gay man and that the assistant pastor was a woman priest. We also felt that God knows our hearts and loves us just as much no matter what church we join. We had long ceased to believe some of what we were taught growing up in the pre-Vatican II days, especially the no longer promulgated maxim that "there is no salvation outside the Roman Catholic Church."

After we made the St. Marguerite faith community our new spiritual home, I volunteered to select the hymns and have used my limited guitar-strumming skills to accompany them at each Sunday liturgy. Al took on a new ministry preparing discussion material for dialogue discussions held after the common meal and socialization time that followed each Sunday liturgy. Each week he selected passages from literature about evolutionary theology (by writers such as Ilia Delio and Diarmuid O'Murchu) or creation spirituality (by writers like Richard Rohr and Matthew Fox) and led the Sunday discussions. He started out introducing our new faith community to *Tomorrow's Catholic: Understanding God and Jesus in a New Millenium* by Michael Morwood (1997: 23rd Publications, Bayard, Mystic CT), an author we knew personally. This book provided an overview of the issues and challenges facing the Catholic Church in today's world and helped open the minds and hearts of the participants to new insights about their faith and more positive views about what it means to be a Christian in today's world.

The first edition of Al's book was instrumental in bringing an interesting woman into our St. Marguerite faith community. Carmen, a retired oncologist, first met Al when he and I were sitting at the Anthem Authors Club table presenting his book to interested passersby at a craft fair that took place in the Sun City Anthem community center. Later we learned that Carmen was born in China, and also lived in Taiwan before coming to the United States. She had practiced Buddhism in her youth, and then became an Episcopalian before converting to Catholicism. Carmen had been attending a local Roman Catholic Church but was looking for a more nurturing faith community.

Carmen bought a copy of Al's book that day. As soon as she finished reading it, she became a regular participant in our St. Marguerite Sunday liturgies and discussion sessions and was a very welcome addition to our faith community. She revered Al and always showed him the deepest respect. For example, despite Al's protests, she always addressed him as "Father Al."

In September 2023, the Reformed Catholic Church held its biannual synod in Las Vegas. During this event, the presiding bishop presented a certificate of induction into the Honorary Order of St. Mychal Judge to Al (posthumously) and to me in recognition of distinguished service to God's people and the Church. It was an unexpected and moving acknowledgment of our contributions to the St. Marguerite Faith Community. (St. Mychal Judge was a Catholic chaplain for New York City firefighters and one of the first responders who died on 9/11 while ministering to them as they tried to save as many lives as possible).

Al's Health Decline

Al was diagnosed with atrial fibrillation, a heart arrhythmia, in the late 1980s when we lived in Wisconsin. Except for needing to be on blood thinners to prevent complications, the A-fib didn't significantly affect his daily life. However, he also developed congestive heart failure which gradually worsened after 2000 and resulted mainly in him having decreased energy for daily activities.

The only acute health episode he experienced prior to 2016 was a brief hospitalization for pneumonia in 2006. Al later recounted that, during that hospitalization, he received a clear message from his deceased mother that he was not going to die!

Al was always grateful to have me accompany him to his doctor visits, since my nursing background enabled me to translate what the doctors said into language he could understand.

Things changed in November 2016 when Al started to feel terrible, with symptoms of restlessness, insomnia, poor appetite, and intermittent fevers. His lab reports revealed that the inflammation marker levels in his blood were sky high. In December he was admitted to the hospital and, after many medical consultations and further testing, the diagnosis arrived at was: "unspecified auto-immune disease." Al's lab results resembled those of someone with Lupus Erythematosus, but his signs and symptoms didn't fit that diagnostic category.

Al was put on a high dose of prednisone and soon felt much better. However, we couldn't get the dosage of prednisone below 20 milligrams per day over the ensuing months without his symptoms recurring.

During Spring 2017 Al experienced three crushed vertebrae, a painful and debilitating side effect of the prednisone. I remember having to pay very close attention to proceeding over any bumps in the road when driving him to medical appointments because of the pain any jolting caused him. Thankfully, two kyphoplasty procedures and a nerve block relieved his back pain.

I was desperate for Al to be weaned off the prednisone responsible for his crushed vertebrae and felt that conventional medicine had nothing to offer him in this regard. So, in June 2017 Al was seen by Dr. Ian Yamane, an Integrative Medicine specialist.

After evaluating his condition, Dr. Yamane put Al on a detoxification regimen, and then a carefully designed treatment plan to promote healing at the cellular level. It included carefully selected supplements and a strict organic, ketogenic, gluten-free diet.

This new diet required me to learn new ways of food shopping and preparation and, initially, was quite a challenge. But positive results came quickly. Al was able to discontinue the prednisone with no recurrence of his symptoms in three months. Since he was a bit of a "chocoholic", Al was grateful to able to still enjoy organic, very dark chocolate in limited amounts!

Al felt that Dr. Yamane's care had both saved his life and restored quality to his daily living. He remained under Dr. Yamane's care for the next five years.

During this time, I had to take over the driving because Al also developed cervical kyphosis, a condition which prevented him from holding his head up and made it difficult for him to see where he was going. In 2017 cervical fusion surgery helped him hold his head higher. But he was still not able to hold his head high enough or turn his head from side to side quickly enough for safe driving.

Al had a more aggressive style of driving than I did, so it was difficult for him to put up with my more tentative approach. But he graciously accepted the situation and seldom complained about it—except when I wouldn't speed up a bit to get though an intersection before the yellow light turned red!

The only other times his "Mr. Crabby" persona showed up briefly was when he felt I was being stingy about the amount of organic maple syrup I allowed him on his gluten-free pancakes. In my defense, I had to limit his carbs to keep him in a state of mild ketosis.

Al had been followed by the same cardiologist, Dr. John Bowers, since moving to Nevada. Dr. Bowers kept tabs on the gradual weakening of his heart for over 20 years. During one office visit, Dr. Bowers told us that his job was to keep Al going until some other health problem caused his demise. This, however, did not turn out to be the case.

Al was scheduled to have a pacemaker inserted in late June 2022, but a fall at home in early June resulted in his being admitted to the hospital. After establishing that Al had not sustained a head injury— only a scalp laceration—the emergency room clinicians focused their concern on his very slow heart rate (40 beats per minute). He was admitted to intensive care and a pacemaker was inserted a day or two later.

After the procedure Al's body became very edematous due to the IV fluids he received. The physicians had to be very careful over the next several weeks in their efforts to eliminate the excessive fluid while maintaining Al's blood pressure within acceptable limits.

Despite not feeling very well, Al was a model hospital patient—appreciative of everything that was being done for him and doing his best to cooperate in his care. His main activity was moving from bed to chair with a daily walk in the hall aided by a physical therapist. I tried to help him pass the time with conversation and a few card games when he felt up to it. Ann and her husband Jim were wonderful supports throughout this difficult time and daughter Lisa came up from San Diego to offer further support.

At one point the discharge plan was to transfer Al to a rehabilitation facility, but the persistent edema scrapped that idea. After several weeks of their best efforts to treat Al's edema and monitor his heart, the doctors finally shared with us the difficult news that Al's heart had become so weak that it could give out at any time. They recommended that he go home under hospice care.

Hospice care was quickly arranged and a hospital bed was placed in our second bedroom. Ann brought a single bed to place beside it so I could sleep in the same room with Al in case he needed any help during the night. He had already been using a motorized chair to get around the house and now continued to do so (with a few scratches and gashes in the baseboards and doorways to prove it! And now for me to remember him by!).

It was so good to have Al home and to have the support of the hospice nurse and the nursing assistants who helped him shower and maintain his personal hygiene. By this time it was early July. I resumed preparing his organic, ketogenic, gluten-free meals. We watched the news and some of our favorite TV programs together, worked a little on jigsaw puzzles and resumed playing cards after dinner.

Al was in good spirits and seemed to be doing quite well during the twelve days following his difficult hospitalization. He minded feeling so weak and needing help with so many activities of daily living, but accepted his situation graciously and always expressed appreciation for everything that was being done for him.

While Al was very weak physically, he remained strong spiritually—supported by his faith, hope and love relationship with the Divine Presence in whom he lived and moved and had his being (a paraphrasing of 2 Corinthians 9-10 and Acts 17:28). And he was looking forward to celebrating his 90th birthday in October 2022.

Al's Final "Falling Upward"

After dinner on the evening of July 12, 2022 Al remarked that he would like to have an office-type chair on wheels at the table where he worked on his jigsaw puzzles. I looked on Amazon.com and found a chair that looked like it would work and the price was right. When I mentioned this to him, Al said he thought that a smaller office chair without arms that we already had in our study would suffice. Since I didn't think that chair would be sturdy or safe enough, I suggested bringing it out to the table so he could try sitting on it and see what he thought before I ordered the other chair from Amazon. Little did I know what was to follow!

Al rode over to the jigsaw puzzle table on his motorized chair. And, as I helped him make the transfer from the motorized chair to the office chair I had brought from the study, his upper body slumped forward and I felt the life flow out of him.

I never doubted that he had just left me to go to a better place—to experience God's unconditional love more directly than we can in this world—but I was also stunned! Thank goodness my iPhone was within reach so I could call Ann and Jim for help, while holding Al so he wouldn't fall onto the floor. I will never forget what an awesome, though painful, experience it was to feel the life force leave his body.

Throughout the slow decline of his health during the first 16 years of his retirement, then the increasing severity of his health problems during the next six years, and finally all he went through in his last hospitalization and the twelve days back home under hospice care, Al hardly ever complained. He still had a sense of humor and accepted all the care he received with sincere appreciation.

His prayer life and trust in the Divine Presence had sustained him and helped him to keep "falling upward"—transforming all the losses he experienced into opportunities to open himself more to God's love. In a largely "first-half-of-life culture" concerned with ego questions of surviving successfully, making money, and being important or significant—Al was able to move beyond those ego-driven questions to questions of the soul in his "journey to joy." My hope is that the readers of this book will gain insights that help them to move forward on their own "journeys to joy."

Here are some tributes that family and friends included in the many sympathy cards received after Al's passing that give witness to the positive way Al lived out his "journey to joy":

From Rauckhorst nieces and nephews:

- Uncle Ronald was truly a great role model—compassionate, calm, understanding and always willing to listen. He followed the path of Jesus, the Great Counselor.
- Uncle Ronald was such a kind man. I was blessed to have him for an uncle. The world has lost a precious soul.
- Uncle Ronald had such an attitude of peace about him. The House of Rauckhorst in heaven just gained another card player!

From close Friends:

- Al had a wonderful life and he truly made the world a better place.
- We loved Al so much. Playing cards and talking about Vatican Council II with him were such special times for us.
- The Speeding Theatre-Over 55 folks will all miss Al and that warm, sweet way of his. He was such a joy and I'm glad we had the wonderful experience of being in the *Jack Benny Isn't 39 Anymore* play with him just a few months before he passed.
- Like swans that mate for life, the love you and Al share is timeless and goes beyond all borders, including death. I feel you will be together forever.
- Al (Ronald) was a good man who understood the treasure of true love. I am forever grate-

ful for Al's wisdom and his great sense of humor. May his beautiful soul be forever singing, dancing and laughing in the presence of our loving God.

- In the short time I knew Al, I came to respect and admire him. I loved the zest for life you both shared. It was like a beacon of hope for all of us still walking on our life journey.

Postscript

Soon after Al's passing, Suzanne (the medium Al wrote about in Chapter Six) told me that he had communicated to her from the other side that he had been given the title "rabbi" (or teacher). That made sense to those who knew him, because it meant that his talents and loving spirit were being put to good use in guiding other souls to open to the divine light and love on the other side. A bit later Suzanne told me about a young woman she had cared for in her midwifery practice who had committed suicide after giving birth and giving up the baby for adoption. She added that Al had helped this young woman to cross over to the other side.

I've only had one reading with Suzanne since Al's passing, during which he communicated some messages related to my efforts to promote his book and prepare this second edition. Over the past year, Suzanne has not done readings for people at all because she has been facing some serious health problems. The process of being a conduit for communication between souls who have passed over and their earthly loved ones requires more energy than Suzanne could afford to expend. Otherwise, I am sure that she would have been relaying to me more messages from Al.

Rebecca, a dear friend of both Al and Suzanne, had been using a meditation technique to synchronize the right and left sides of the brain for five or six years. This synchronization process increases the brain waves that slow thoughts down, and this opens the meditator up to an expanded state of consciousness. This friend had learned to use this method to connect with souls who have passed and are in a healing center on the other side. So, while meditating two days after Al passed, she found herself in a healing center on the other side where souls who have just passed over are helped to become unstuck from their earthly traumas and blockages.

Rebecca reported having a very joyous meeting with Al there. His soul was in the process of being cleared of some dense earth energy that tunes out love and light. He communicated to her that he was ecstatic, feeling awesome, and that he would be teaching other souls, helping them with their transition to life on the other side. This was consistent with Suzanne telling me that Al had communicated to her that he had been given the title "rabbi", which means teacher or scholar.

Our daughter, Lisa, also has intuitive gifts and sometimes senses the presence of spirits and sees auras (the energy fields around living things). For example, after Maizey (our 22 year old cat) died in 2017, Lisa sensed Maizey's presence in our home when she visited us. More recently, Lisa told me that she was sure her dad turned on the television a couple of times to give her enough light to gather the dog leashes she needed for her very early morning walks with her four dogs. She also once visualized her dad's spirit waving to her animatedly, but she was unable to understand any message he may have been trying to convey.

When Lisa visited me during the 2023 holiday season, she mentioned being sure that her dad was very busy and "having a ball" on the other side and this was why she didn't sense his presence in our home. It astounded me when she told me that, while I was talking on the phone with a friend from my faith community, she could see that individual's golden aura. A gold aura is a sign of spiritual and emotional maturity, wisdom and compassion in a person who radiates positive energy into the world. This description definitely fit this woman's sunny, compassionate and generous personality.

Reverend Linda Pilato, the Associate Pastor of the St. Marguerite Faith Community, is another friend who has intuitive gifts and reports having felt Al's presence briefly a number of times since his passing. When Al and I first started participating in St. Marguerite Sunday Masses, Reverend Linda says she felt she already knew us and celebrated in her heart when we decided to become part of this independent Catholic faith community. In January 2024, she shared a homily with us during Mass that she firmly believed was a message from Al. She had felt impelled to write it down and share it with us. The following two paragraphs summarize the main points of that homily.

Christianity should primarily be a *way of life* that follows Jesus the Christ's teachings and example, is supported by a safe, welcoming faith community, and is not primarily an organization or a social club.

Christianity is:

- *A way of life* that doesn't withhold health care from pregnant women until they are close to death and that respects their personhood, as well as that of the fetus.
- *A way of life* that does not fear or discriminate against LGBTQ+ people who should be welcomed to live a Christian way of life.
- *A way of life* that can incorporate many cultural traditions while keeping faith in God.

Coming to church should strengthen us to live a Christian lifestyle, and not be an occasion to wallow in our missteps or tout our accolades. We should all be equal, while having our own strengths. Love needs to be our common ground, not the prayers we say, the hymns we sing, or if we take Holy Communion each week. Christians should not be afraid to grow in their knowledge of God. Their beliefs may change as a result, but they needn't fear that their faith — their relationship with God — will be compromised. There are going to be times when what God's voice tells you will be hard to believe. For example, both Mary and Joseph had to listen to the startling messages God sent them and change their beliefs when she conceived Jesus; and this strengthened their faith — their relationship with God. In this day and age, when things are so uncertain, we need to listen for God's loving voice and then not be afraid to follow where it leads.

The main thrust of this homily seemed to me to indicate that Al's spirit is still very much aware of the many struggles regarding peace and justice going on in our world today, and that he wanted to remind us of important messages he included in *Journey to Joy*. I would love to be open to communication from Al on the other side—but I tend to have a very busy "monkey" mind which doesn't give him much room to come through. I am at peace, with the assurances I have had from Suzanne, Rebecca, Lisa, and Reverend Linda that Al is very busy on the other side helping other souls to open themselves to God's amazing, unconditional love! And, when my time comes, I am sure that Al will be there to help me cross over to join all the saints and angels seeing our loving God face to face, knowing Him/Her directly, and sharing in heaven's everlasting peace and joy.